Astrology Tarot Spirit

musings along the mystics path

Volume 1

Noel Eastwood

All rights reserved copyright © Noel Eastwood 2020

All rights reserved, copyright © 2020 Noel Eastwood
Noel Eastwood asserts the moral right to be identified as the author of this work. By payment of the required fees, you have been granted the non-exclusive and non-transferable right to access and read the text of this ebook on screen or in print form. No part of the text may be reproduced, transmitted, downloaded, decompiled, reverse engineered, stored in or introduced into any information storage or retrieval system, in any form or by any means, electronic or mechanical, known or otherwise yet invented, without the express permission of Noel Eastwood.

Tarot deck illustrations from the original Arthur Edward Waite, *The Pictorial Key To The Tarot* (1911), illustrated by Pamela Colman-Smith.

All work in this book is by Noel Eastwood unless otherwise stated.

Direct all correspondence to: Noel Eastwood
Email: info@plutoscave.com
Web: www.plutoscave.com
Facebook - @PlutosCave
Illustration: Anthony Jones
Cover illustration: Rock
Web: https://www.fiverr.com/inbox/rock_0407

Table of Contents

Author's preface

Chapter 1 - The Mythology of Capricorn and the Winter Solstice by Noel Eastwood

Chapter 2 - The Four Elements As Keys to understanding your child

Chapter 3 - Is there a way to see my spiritual path in my astrology chart?

Chapter 4 - Psychotherapy and spirituality in astrology

Chapter 5 - Greek mythology and personal myth making

Chapter 6 – Excerpt: The Fool's Journey through the Tarot Major Arcana

Chapter 7 - Is there love in my astrology chart?

Chapter 8 - The Aries Myth and the Spring Equinox

Chapter 9 - Psychology, the brain and biofeedback

Chapter 10 - The mystics path – 1

Chapter 11 - The mystics path - 2

Chapter 12 - Bringing back the dead

Chapter 13 - Life after death

Chapter 14 - Excerpt: The Fool's Journey Through The Tarot Pentacles – The Ace of Pentacles

Chapter 15 - We live in two worlds

Chapter 16 - Tarot Scrying Meditation - The Hierophant

Chapter 17 - The Asteroid Goddesses - Ceres / Demeter

Chapter 18 - My black blob experience

Chapter 19 - Astrology cycles

Chapter 20 - Stopping the world

Chapter 21 - Dr Carl Jung - an introduction

Chapter 22 - Astrology and family therapy

Chapter 23 - A quickie reading at a boat party

Chapter 24 - Emotional self defence—rock, water + boundaries

Chapter 25 - Except: 'Astrology of Health: physical and psychological health in the natal and progressed charts'. Earth Dominance in Health

Chapter 26 – Astrology, psychology and epilepsy

About the author

Author's preface

These volumes are an edited and expanded compilation derived from my Pluto's Cave newsletters available only to my subscribers. They incorporate the great passions of my life: astrology, tarot, taoist meditation and depth or Jungian psychology. Now that I am retired from my psychology practice I have more time to share my understanding of the mystic's path in my newsletters, books, teaching and in mentoring students and professionals.

I began my psychology studies soon after I finished my teaching career. At that time I had a clinical hypnotherapy and biofeedback practice, taught tai chi twice a week and ran regular astrology and meditation classes, I was a busy fellow.

My first book, 'Psychological Astrology and the Twelve Houses', was published in 2015. I have since written several books covering such topics as self hypnosis, meditation, psychopathology, astral travel, astrology, archetypes, tarot, education and health.

Writing newsletters such as these is a means of teaching the esoteric and psychological basis of meditation, astrology and tarot. For instance, my *Fool's Journey Through The Tarot* series is designed to educate while it entertains. The *Fool's Journey* series illustrate how each of the 78 cards in your tarot deck can be used for personal growth along the mystics path. It has surprised me that this series has sparked a lot of interest in those interested in personal growth as well as in tarot.

I believe that those who seek a deeper meaning of life beyond what is told to us on the 6 o'clock news, are mystics on the path of knowledge. To that effect these volumes are dedicated to you. I am sure that you will enjoy my musings, musings along the mystics path.

If you would like to subscribe to my free newsletters or online course please visit my web site www.plutoscave.com

Please join me and many others in this adventure of self discovery and growth.

Noel Eastwood

November 2020

Australia

"An unexamined life is not worth living."
From *Plato's Apology,* quoted from the speech Socrates, the Greek philosopher, gave at his trial.

http://www.sparknotes.com/philosophy/apology/section7.rhtml

Chapter 1 - The Mythology of Capricorn and the Winter Solstice

The arrival of Capricorn announces the Winter Solstice, midwinter's day, the shortest day of the year in the northern hemisphere. People in Europe and the Middle East celebrated this day which heralded the sun's return. This day announced the coming of warmth, sunshine and the wealth of produce at harvest. Here in the southern hemisphere we celebrate the Summer Solstice, midsummer's day, a time when we embrace the start of our glorious summer holidays.

The Winter Solstice marks the sun's victory in the celestial dance of the seasons swinging between the privations of winter and the bounty of summer. It heralds the end of winter's long, cold nights, boredom, depression, limited food choices and inactivity. There was always the spectre of starvation as our ancestor's stores of food threatened to run out towards the end of winter.

Several pagan gods of interest to astrologers were celebrated at the Winter Solstice: Sol Invictus, Mithrais and Saturnalia (Saturn). Sol Invictus was elevated to God status in Rome in 274 AD. Sol Day or Sunday, was decreed by the Roman Emperor Constantine in 321 AD. An illustration of how important the Winter Solstice was to our ancestors is seen in the label given to the solar god, Mithrais. Mithraism was the most popular pre-Christian religion of the Roman Empire. At that time the Winter Solstice was called: "the birth day of the unconquered sun". This was the day when Mithrais emerged from his cave, or birth place, witnessed by two shepherds.

The festival of Saturnalia deserves mention as it was one of the major celebrations of the pre Christian era. Saturnalia is of course, Saturn, who, back in ancient Roman and Greek times, was primarily revered as a god of agriculture. The Roman festival of Saturnalia was held from the 17th - 25th December. It was a time to celebrate the Winter Solstice. The courts were closed as no one could be punished for harming people or property during this week long festival.

"In Roman mythology, Saturn was an agricultural deity who was said to have reigned over the world in the Golden Age, when humans enjoyed the spontaneous bounty of the earth without labour in a state of innocence. The revelries of Saturnalia were supposed to reflect the conditions of the lost mythical age... As a deity of agricultural bounty, Saturn embodied prosperity and wealth in general... Unlike several Roman religious festivals which were particular to cult sites in the city, the prolonged seasonal celebration of Saturnalia at home could be held anywhere in the Empire. Saturnalia continued as a secular celebration long after it was removed from the official calendar. As William Warde Fowler notes: "'[Saturnalia] has left its traces and found its parallels in great numbers of medieval and modern customs, occurring about the time of the winter solstice.'"
https://en.wikipedia.org/wiki/Saturnalia

Saturn, as we know, rules Capricorn, as such it holds a special place in astrology as the active and forthright Cardinal Earth sign. The links between Saturn, the celebrations of Saturnalia, Sol Invictus, Mithraism, Christianity and the myths of Capricorn, calls for closer examination. Jack Finegan in 'Myth & Mystery: An

Introduction to the Pagan Religions of the Biblical World' (1989) writes: *"...But the worship of the sun-god continued widely throughout the empire, and under Aurelian (A.D. 270- 275) the cult was restored to its former high estate. In the year 274 Aurelian declared the god - now called Deus Sol Invictus - the official deity of the Roman Empire; he built a splendid temple of the sun in Rome... and set the sun's birthday celebration (naturalis solis invicti) on December 25th, the date then accepted for the Winter Solstice (also in his solar character was the God Mithrais). In the time of Constantine the cult of Deus Sol Invictus was still at its height, and the portrait of the sun god was on the coins of Constantine....Likewise it must have been in this time and with the intent to transform the significance of an existing sacred date that the birthday of Jesus, which had been celebrated in the East on January 6th... was placed in Rome on December 25th, the date of the birth of Sol Invictus. This date appears in a list of dates probably compiled in A.D. 336 and published in the Roman city calendar."* (Finegan, p. 211-212).

The upper half of the Capricorn glyph shows the head and torso of a goat. This, perhaps, reflects the goat's tendency to climb to higher ground where it can gain a better view of the landscape to locate food and avoid predators. Its lower half shows the tail of a fish linking it to water and spirituality. Thus we might say that one half of Capricorn is related to our conscious mind and the other half to our unconscious. Perhaps the ancient astrologers intended for Capricorn to symbolise our ascent to the peak of human achievement while remaining spiritually grounded.

There are a number of myths this complex sign draws upon:

Amalthia, a sea-goat nymph, was the baby Zeus' nurse (nanny). His mother, Rhea, hid Zeus in a cave to protect him from his father, Cronus, who was in the habit of eating his babies. We use the word 'nanny' as the label we give to a mother goat as well as to a child's female carer when the mother is absent. When Amalthia assisted Zeus to rescue his siblings he placed her in the heavens as the constellation of Capricorn. The word 'Capricorn' means goat (caper) and horn (cornu). The magical horn of Amalthia was taken by Zeus and was known as the 'Horn of Plenty'.

The Babylonian goddess, Ea, watched over the land by day but at night she returned to the oceans. Her upper half was of a goat and the lower half a fish.

Around 5,000 BC in Sumer and Babylon, their god, **Enki**, was represented as a satyr as well as a sea-goat. He was also known as the god of nature which is the same designation as the Greek god, Pan. Both Pan and Enki were known to bring life to the fields.

The god, Pan, was the son of Hermes, he ruled shepherds and nature (animals, the soil and trees). Pan was part goat and part human. I think that Pan is the best fit for Capricorn.

Aegipan was one of the Panes. Panes were goat-legged shepherds of ancient Greece said to be descended from the god, Pan. In one version of the Capricorn myth there appears a deadly monster, Typhon, who viciously flung Zeus' body parts into a river. Aegipan transformed into part goat and part fish to rescue the body parts and returned them to Zeus. He was rewarded by being placed in the skies as the constellation of Capricorn. Aegipan's name means Goat-Pan.

Another Greek myth involves Pricus, the king of the magical sea-goats. When his children crawled onto the land they would lose their fish tails and transform into ordinary goats. King Pricus had a special magic, he could reverse time. It seemed that whenever he turned his back on his children they would crawl onto the beaches and turn into hairy goats. He was constantly rescuing his children by rewinding time to before they climbed onto the beach. Eventually he gave up, kids are inquisitive and impossible to control. Eventually Pricus lost all of his children and became a lonely king. He asked the God of Time, Cronus, to let him die. Cronus placed him in the heavens as the constellation of Capricorn. From there he could watch his children climbing to the highest peaks of the mountains below.

This article appeared in the December 2018 edition of the **Federation of Australian Astrologers** journal, Vol. 48, No. 4.

Chapter 2 - The Four Elements As Keys to understanding your child

This is as an introduction to the presentation I gave to students at the International Astrology Academy in October 2019. You can download the full 4 lesson presentations at their website (https://www.astrocollege.org/) : Psychological Astrology of Babies, Children and Teenagers.

The element of Water illustrates the traits and qualities of Freud's Oral Stage of Psychosexual Development. It defends against abandonment, betrayal, emotional rejection and loneliness by attaching and connecting to others and love objects. Attachments such as pets, cigarettes, food, soft toys, even houses and other significant objects like a car. In particular it involves love and emotional connections: *"I need you, please don't leave me! I can't live without you."*

Air illustrates Denial traits and qualities. It defends against confusion, ambivalence and restricted freedom of expression by denying that anything is wrong, by dissociating and escaping into fantasy instead of facing the real issue. Air people often escape into intellectual explanations and magical thinking: *"It's an omen so I don't have to go to counselling now. I know how to handle this situation. If I just ignore it, it will go away. The aliens will save us."*

Earth illustrates Anal traits and qualities. It defends against change and insecurity by exerting control, often through power struggles with authority figures, digging their heels in, and by hoarding and collecting. Earth people struggle to let go: *"I'm not shifting! I can't handle change, it makes me feel anxious and insecure."*

Fire illustrates Oedipal traits and qualities. It defends against insignificance, inertia, personal meaninglessness, impotence, criticism, rivalry, jealousy and envy, vulnerability and humiliation. Feeling ignored and worthless leads to competing with others for attention: *"Hey, look at me! Pick me, I'm the best one, pick me!"*

You can also examine the house and sign placement of the two luminaries, Sun and Moon, as they can represent the child's Father and Mother. They also illustrate cultural father and mother Archetypes. These are powerful forces in your psyche, astrologers spend a great deal of time learning to understand these two foundational archetypes in the chart.

I recommend that you read as many of Liz Greene and Howard Sasportas' books as you can find. Liz and Howard provide an alternative astrological explanation to Freud's stages of Psychosexual Development, their books are a 'must have' for psychologically oriented astrologers.

Key significators in a child's chart include: elemental dominance, chart signature, focal planets, sign and house dominance (these are explained in greater detail in the course mentioned above as well as in my books and later newsletters).

Attachment and parenting

Your style of parenting may contribute to your child's evolving and developing personality.

Overly permissive parents: these parents fail to realise that they are the adult and the child is just a child. As adults they are responsible for making decisions that affect their child's emotional development. A child has no understanding of nutrition and so when given a choice of what to eat they simply don't know what is best for them. When you ask your child to choose what they want for lunch is an invitation for them to make uninformed food choices. A parent in this category has often had issues with their own upbringing and don't want to be like their own parents. However, they are adults and they need to understand that making a wise choice is one thing that small children will always struggle with. This parenting style may contribute to raising a child who does not know how to take turns, to share things and they may even become school bullies. In later years they may struggle to make wise and responsible choices.

Unstructured parents and exposure to domestic violence: these parents have often experienced negative parental role models that includes membership of gangs, exposure to drugs, sexualised behaviour and violence on TV, video games by the parents themselves or their visitors. Poor role models may contribute to a child developing attachment issues such as aggression, sexualised and predatory behaviour, oppositional behaviour and defiance, inability to form friendships and relationships as well as manipulative interactions with others as they grow into adults.

Some may even end up in court for acting immorally and irresponsibly.

A balanced upbringing is certainly helped when both parents are emotionally balanced. Setting boundaries and limits to demands can train a child to self-regulate their impulses which is what is required in later years when they become adults. These issues of parenting are discussed in greater detail in the lessons that this presentation came from at https://www.astrocollege.org/ : Psychological Astrology of Babies, Children and Teenagers. They can also be found in later newsletters and in my books.

NOTE: not every child who experiences the above parenting styles will turn out with emotional or behavioural difficulties. In fact very few do, but this is something we should all be aware of. Neither do hard aspects in a child's chart manifest them in a negative way. Personality development is far more complex than that. The charts in this course help highlight what to look for but they cannot explain every detail of someone's personality. The important thing to remember is that each point in the chart tells the astrologer something important. It is up to the experienced astrologer to determine if these aspects manifest in a positive or a negative way. Some of the most wonderful people have horrific charts. It is up to you, the professional astrologer, to gain an understanding of human personality and how it is written in the stars.

Presented by Noel Eastwood at the IAA in October 2019.

Chapter 3 - Is there a way to see my spiritual path in my astrology chart?

This question came from a conversation I had with a subscriber about astrology and spirituality - can astrology show someone's spiritual path?

As far as I am concerned the answer is a definite 'Yes'. The problem is that it is not one single point, it is the synthesis of the entire chart. Yes, there are pointers and as a psychologist I always look for conflict and elemental dominance in the chart to guide me. These clearly highlight the native's spiritual path.

There are certain astrological signatures such as a luminary (Sun and Moon) conjunct or opposed by an outer planet. These are high on the list that guides me to see someone's spiritual or life purpose.

For instance, someone with Pluto conjunct Sun shows this person is incarnating to find internal peace and meaning. They live with insecurity each day until they come to terms with their fears. They are learning to manage life's ups and downs through applying a large degree of self control, in this lifetime. Their spiritual destiny for this lifetime, therefore, is to learn self control to gain inner peace and harmony.

However, Pluto conjunct Sun has many other features besides self control. It also involves such things as astral travel, flying in dreams, lucid dreaming, energy healing, kundalini. So yes, this person's destiny is to learn self control, but they can also access Pluto's special powers along the way. What most fail to understand is that they must first earn the right to access and use that power.

This is where mentoring, psychotherapy and specific meditation forms comes into the picture. Learning to let go emotionally and to engage your power at a deep psychological level becomes your focus in this lifetime. Understanding that Pluto rules the unconscious can help in this process. This is where a well trained astrologer with a background in psychology can contribute in a big way.

Now we move to the sign the Sun is in which adds a special layer to the native's life purpose. If the Sun is in an Earth sign it suggests this person is learning to ground their life, to manifest change and bring power into reality, to make things real.

If in an Air sign it suggests intellectual change and transformation, she seeks to bring power through knowledge to communicate this to get her message across to the masses.

In Fire it is personal growth, to transform personally and creatively. This may be as a teacher, a musician, an actor, writer, leader or an orator.

In Water it involves coming to terms with emotional experiences. One thing they need to do is control their emotions in relationships and to then come to terms with their own sense of betrayal and abandonment. They seek, if other aspects are present in their chart, to convey this sense of security to others.

The next layer is the House in which these two planets reside. There are 12 of them and I won't go into this right now, that's an entire course in itself, or you can go online to purchase my book, "Psychological Astrology And The twelve Houses".

Chapter 4 - Psychotherapy and spirituality in astrology

I'll continue with the spiritual path in astrology and add some psychology to illustrate how I use the chart in my psychotherapy practice.

In the previous chapter I explained how the Sun is one of the pointers to spirituality in the chart. I also said that there is no single point, spirituality is a complex synthesis of the entire chart. In this chapter I will show you a simple meditation I do and what I teach some of my students when they wish to take that step along their spiritual path.

Take out your chart, if you don't have one please go to www.chartsubscriber.com and create one for free. Look for your Sun and note what sign it is in (your Sun sign is your birth sign, like a Leo or Virgo); look at the house it is in (1st, 9th, 11th, etc.) and note if there are any conjunctions or oppositions (planets next to it by 10 degrees or directly opposite).

It is important to note that the planetary archetypes don't have a fixed gender, they can be either male, female, no gender or both at once.

The inner world is a funny place and with practice you'll see why it is such an amazing world. For instance, the Sun is generally male, for some cultures it is female. For some people, especially if the mother is the dominant parent, it is female. Don't be surprised that over time and with a lot of practice, your archetype's gender changes.

Close your eyes and imagine that you can walk up to your Sun and talk to him. For most of us the deeper you go into the light trance state the easier this becomes. Ask your Sun questions about anything you like. Next, ask him to take your hands in his and to send all his light and love into you. Feel his energy and where he sends it into your body. When you are ready ask him how he might help you along your spiritual path.

Next invite any planet that is conjunct or opposed your Sun to join you both and then dialogue with the two of them. Find out what conflicts they experience and what they have in common.

For some people this is easy, for others it isn't. If you are struggling just keep doing and practice your relaxation or mindfulness daily. One day it will just happen for you.

Chapter 5 - Greek mythology and personal myth making

I often hear people say: *'I want to be an astrologer',* but I think to myself, *'If only you knew how much study and practice goes into becoming a professional astrologer you just might change your mind.'*

As we all know that anything of value is worth your best effort and so becoming an astrologer is certainly worth your best.

Psychological astrology is a relatively new branch of astrology. Considering that astrology is thousands of years old we could almost say that psychological astrology is brand new. Psychological astrology aims to describe human personality, our drives, urges and instincts. The great Swiss psychiatrist, Dr Carl Jung, was so taken with astrology that he created his own hand drawn charts for himself and his patients.

This is perhaps one of the most important statements I can make to a beginner astrologer: if you want to be an exceptional astrologer then study Greek mythology. There you will find the roots of psychology and astrology.

These myths illustrate the many personality traits that you can see in your family, friends and acquaintances. The desires, jealousies, urges and fears are all there. In each myth you will see people striving to understand life through action and conflict. Some psychologists, like myself, use myth in our sessions. They make powerful metaphors to help explore and explain a person's life journey.

Another way you can use myth is through personal narrative or story telling. These stories are your '*personal myths*'. You live a life of myth and by telling your '*story*' you can examine your personal myths – beliefs, attitudes and values. Sometimes you will find links to the myths of ancient Greece in your narratives and those of your clients. Astrology then becomes enlivened with personal experience.

Can I suggest that you do your research and read up on the Greek myths associated with your astrology signs and planets? Then write down your life as a story, just like a myth or fairy tale. You can even start with, *"Once upon a time there was a little boy/girl who..."*

Put it down and come back to it the next day and examine the themes that flow through your story, see if you can find links to the astrological myths we use today. Do any of your personal myth themes sound like anything in your chart?

This process is fascinating and one you can do again and again for each period of your life. If you enjoy this I am sure that you will love examining your personal myths using the tarot archetypes.

Chapter 6 – Excerpt: The Fool's Journey through the Tarot Major Arcana

The **Fool's Journey series** by Noel Eastwood

The Fool

Innocence; folly; spontaneity; faith; trust; beginning.

"The true Tarot is symbolism; it speaks no other language and offers no other signs. Given the inward meaning of its emblems, they do become a kind of alphabet which is capable of indefinite combinations and makes true sense in all." Arthur Edward Waite, The Pictorial Key to the Tarot (1911).

"The fool doth think he is wise, but the wise man knows himself to be a fool." William Shakespeare, *As You Like It*

From: *The Pictorial Key to the Tarot*, A.E. Waite (1911)

"With light step, as if earth and its trammels had little power to restrain him, a young man in gorgeous vestments pauses at the brink of a precipice among the great heights of the world; he surveys the blue distance before him - its expanse of sky rather than the prospect below... He is a prince of the other world on his travels through this one ... amidst the morning glory, in the keen air. The sun, which shines behind him, knows whence he came, whither he is going, and how he will return by another path after many days. He is the spirit in search of experience."

Along a dusty dirt road in the countryside of the Mystic Isle a youth is walking. He steps out lightly with laughter in his throat and a bright smile on his face. Having left his home and family troubles behind he feels happy, carefree. He effortlessly strides through the countryside for miles and miles.

As he passes the dry stubble of a harvested wheat field he spies an old scarecrow. He climbs through the timber-railed fence and, stepping carefully over the cut wheat stalks, walks over to the scarecrow.

The scarecrow's clothes are old, the shirt is thin and well worn. It has many ragged holes in it. The Fool gently and carefully, almost reverently, removes the shirt and places it on the ground. Then he takes his own shirt off and puts it respectfully on the scarecrow as though he is dressing his aged grandfather. He steps back, chuckles to himself and puts the scarecrow's worn shirt on his own back and returns to the road.

Later that day, weary and beginning to question the wisdom of his flight from home, the boy finds himself on the edge of the sea cliffs. He puts down his staff and bundle and peers over the edge at the waves crashing below. He stands up again, takes up his staff and bundle and moves on.

―

The group across the channel observes him, pointing him out to those amongst them who had not yet noticed the boy.

"Do we turn him back?" one asks.

"Is he too young?" another adds.

"Is he ready?" from another.

"What do we know of him?" from yet another.

"Ah, 'tis young Follin, native of the Mystic Isle," one of the elders explains. "Fourteen years old. He is but a boy and the burdens at home are such that even his father could not face them."

"So he runs..." another chimes in.

"Just as his father did," says another.

"No, the father ran from failure of his powers, a mixture of pride, guilt and grief. The boy runs from inadequacy and shame. The burden is too great for his young shoulders. He has not yet come to believe in himself. Reflected in the eyes of his family, peers, teachers and elders he sees himself a fool."

"Untapped potential," another murmurs.

"Shall we take him on then?" asks one of the voices.

"But is he too damaged?" questions another.

"Yes, he is disturbed, depressed and sees no future for himself," comes the reply. "He is naive, bullied at school, dyslexic and ignorant of the world beyond..."

"We see his folly, his ignorance, his stumbling and we must ask ourselves: This poor Fool, will he ever succeed in life?" another intones.

Their voices weave through the group: a whisper of wind, a hiss; a grunt of assent; a rising inflection, melodic and true.

"Do we do this for his benefit, his enlightenment, or is it to fulfil our own needs?" another queries.

Suddenly the group turns as one. The boy had jumped from the cliff, or had he just fallen? His body plummets towards the rocks below, still clutching his staff and bundle. Before his feet touch the waves a rainbow appears beneath his feet. His downward momentum ceases and he is propelled forward along the rainbow as if it were a bridge.

The group across the channel disappears and a solitary figure strides down to the shoreline to meet the boy.

—

Follin steps off the rainbow bridge onto the mainland. He naively walks his own path, not knowing where his journey may take him.

Carrying his belongings in a cloth sack, wrapped about a stout staff, he remembers not, nor cares, what it contains. It is just another burden he has to carry through life, or so he thinks. *'Just like the bullying at school and the colour of my hair. Like the shame of having a sick mother I had to care for when I was supposed to be studying. Like my father who left when my brother died. Life is a mystery - and a burden.'*

Follin begins his journey as a naive fool but it will soon become a journey of discovery into himself. Leaving behind all he knows, and ignorant of the consequences of his actions, Follin begins a mystic's journey. Like so many Fools before him, his is a quest for wisdom, knowledge, enlightenment, but he does not know it yet.

This introduces Follin at the start of his journey (Follin is the Old French word for 'Fool'). This first book of the **Fool's Journey series** *describes the initiation of the mystics journey. If you are reading this then you are definitely on the mystics journey too. As Arthur Waite believed, the Tarot is a wonderful guide or pathway to enlightenment. Many of us started our own mystics journey with many of the same issues that Follin had.*

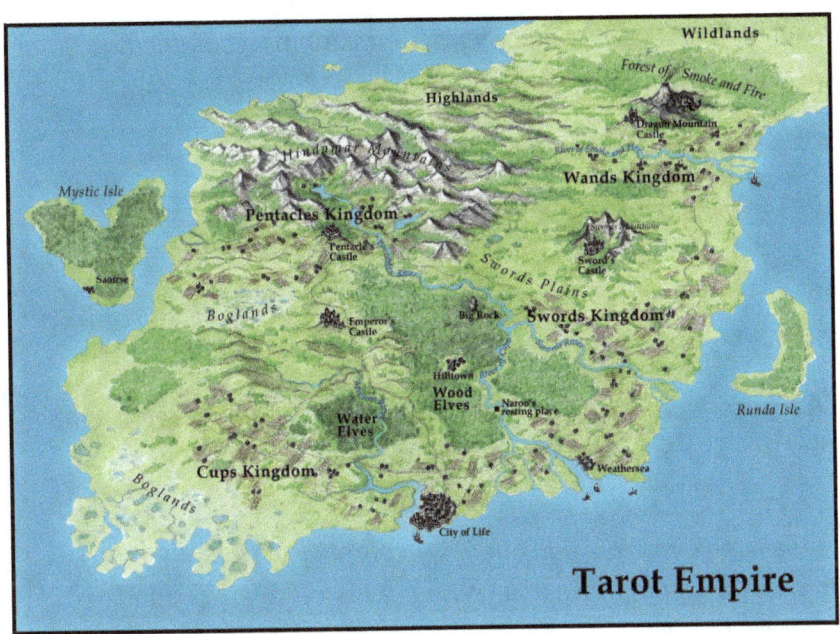

I have endeavoured to weave contemporary themes into my series so that those on the mystic's path can relate to each book. Interspersed throughout the series are specific techniques and meditations to assist you on your journey. I have drawn heavily on my experiences as a psychologist and many years as a meditator to write this series. I have also endeavoured to keep it as close to the spiritual model of the 'mystics journey' as possible. One could liken this series to Joseph Campbell's 'A Hero's Journey'. One would then see Follin as representing the Hero within us all.

Books two (Pentacles), three (Swords), four (Cups) and five (Wands) will take you on an adventure even further into the inner workings of Tarot and your spiritual universe.

You can purchase your copy from Amazon or other online bookstores. It is available in colour as a paperback, from www.bookdepository.com

Also available as an audiobook masterfully narrated by Jonathan Johns.

Reviews

"Amazing journey! By far one of my favorites, the narrator's voice had me fully engaged in the story. Definitely a must have." J

"I really enjoyed this audiobook, and I really wish that the others in the series of the Fool's Journey were also available in audio format." LM

"Wonderful Fairytale version of the Major Arcana. Great listen with the kids, enjoyable & inspiring. Informative on a simple level with a great intro & quote for each card." MT

"I thoroughly enjoyed listening to this book today. The narration is excellent and the content is amazing. It takes you to a deeper understanding of the Major Arcana. I highly recommend this book no matter how experienced or inexperienced a Tarot reader you are!" LY

"I am so glad this was available as an audiobook, it took the story to a whole other level. I really enjoyed the narration & will definitely listen more than once to really tap into the journey as my own. Thank you to the author & narrator." S

"Very insightful audiobook! Gives you a better understanding of the meaning of the fool in the tarot!" ACF

"Thank you for your wonderful books. I'm just finishing the Major Arcana and I'm a convert. Will be purchasing all in the series. Much appreciated." JG

"In October of 2009 Carl Jung's Red Book was released for the first time. Chronicling the great psychoanalyst's venture into his own subconscious, revealing fractal universes and personifications of unconscious material. A whole new world of it's own. One that is not unlike the universal symbology embodied in the Major Arcana of the Tarot. Noel Eastwood's delightful book, "The Fool's Journey through the Tarot Major Arcana," is unlike any other tool for learning about this centuries old symbology and how it can be meditated upon, and used to relate to the workings of our daily lives, and our own subconscious. It is a free-flowing, progressive adventure of the Fool through all of the other cards. Taking the simple Spirit he was conceived with, the Fool advances as he encounters each force and personality. A true "Hero's Journey," and one that every spiritual adventurist will love and recognize. The story sucked me in, and only spat me out at the end. I recommend this series as a companion to the works of Carl Jung, Anna Wise, Joseph Campbell, Paul Foster Case, J. Nigro Sansonese, and my own." FK

"I've read many of Noel's books on Astrology and tarot. I'm always amazed at how easily his writings lend themselves to being transformative to readers at any point along the Tao. His writings present the reader with a systematic approach to psychological and spiritual growth little matched in understanding and ease of use, than by other writers I can think of. If you are looking for a place to begin or enrich your journey, I'd recommend you follow the Fool in his journey through the Tarot." MR

"What a wonderful way to bring an easy and deep understanding of the major arcana. This book was enlightening and entertaining from start to finish. I'm definitely not a tarot student, or teacher. Far from it. But this book makes me want to learn. A whole new world has opened up for me. It's an odd feeling having epiphanies as I read, but that happened. Beautifully written and drawn, The Fool's Journey is a keeper!" KM

"This easy to understand text is not in any way simplistic; it's filled with deep meaning. This book will assist in your inward journey. Use it along with meditation to reach a better understanding of yourself and others." MR

"I really loved this book, I will be buying book 2 and 3 of this series for sure. As I was reading it helped me to reflect on my life and when I've been at each card and gave a lot of deeper meanings and shed some light on some of the cards I don't love to see when pulling for myself. not only that it truly kept me captivated and interested to see how Follin felt after getting to the world. Can't wait for his journey through the pentacles." C

"A magical journey through the tarot! Delightful to read - also, makes the tarot cards easier to learn/remember. I highly recommend this series - whether you are a beginner or advanced tarot reader." AC

"I really liked this story. I really brought to live the major arcana and I think when I pull my cards this narative will make me smile as I reflect. I am very much looking forward to the other stories in the Kingdom of Tarot." MK

"I really enjoyed listening to this audiobook, for me it is insightfull and inspiring, I am using it as a personal leaning aid as I commence my own fools journey, it's powerful and gifted narrative suits my own particular learning style, it also helps give my journey perspective and a sturdy framework, like the tarot." BC

"I have just finished reading this marvelous introduction to the Major Arcana as I followed Follin (The Fool) on his journey through the Tarot Empire. Noel takes a unique (at least to me) method to teaching the meanings of The Major Arcana cards by weaving together an interesting story about a journey taken by Follin. I have always had a rudimentary understanding of the Tarot (mostly through my profession), but thanks to this well told story I have come to see more to the cards then I had imagined existed. I found myself relating to Follin's journey on several levels (which was quite a revelation). Each story unveils new revelations about life to Follin at the same time explaining (in easy to understand prose, much like the use of parables) the meanings to each card. Each card has it's own specific meaning and yet Noel manages to blend them all together into a seamless story. The cards all have interesting contributions to the "journey", my favorite cards were Death, The Hierophant and The Hermit. All in all, from beginning to end I enjoyed this very much and would recommend this read to those who enjoy a good read and/or have an interest in Tarot Major Acana cards." RD

'Greetings. I just finished the Swords book on Follin's quest. If you have a release date for the Cups volume, I'll be more than happy to buy a copy as soon as it hits Amazon kindle. Thank you for writing such tales, they have really helped me understand tarot better. I've been really trying to grasp the essence of Tarot for a few years because I plan to set up office and offer paid readings. And this is not an exaggeration, your books are just what many of us need, as we're usually people that can relate to Follin's struggle... I know for sure because I can actually feel it. Thank you for the awesome gift and the inspiration. You'll hear back from me when I get my much overdue success, and I'll make sure to honor your work through my own, and thanks again for bringing Follin to life.' AM

"I am really looking forward to the Cups book. I've listened to the Fools Journey 5 times, its starting to sink in very well. You are an amazingly gifted writer to have come up with this story and have given the tarot a voice words cannot describe my admiration. I am so grateful you crossed my path to help me understand these complex subjects, thank you." CM

Chapter 7 - Is there love in my astrology chart?

Love is something that comes up time and again in astrology readings and on the astrology forums. Like spirituality, love is complex and synthesised from the entire chart not just one or two points. We generally look at Venus and the 7th house but it is way more than just these two points.

Love is not just *romantic love*, it is probably best described by the word *'nurture'*. To love is to nurture. The sentence: *'I love you and I want you to love me,'* is very close to this sentence: *'I nurture you and I wish you to nurture me'*. The word, *'nurture'* is a powerful and evocative word.

Your first love is your mother. You are part of her, inseparable in time, space and feeling, for 9 months. After birth mother continues to nurture you for another period of time, usually around 9 months before weaning onto solid food. Nurturing, therefore, becomes one of your first keys to who you love and how you love. This is represented by your Moon, its sign, its house placement and any aspects it makes to other planets particularly conjunct or opposite. The Moon shows how you nurture and how you like to be nurtured as well as how you nurture yourself.

Now it gets complicated because I've added:

(1) how you nurture others

(2) how you like to be nurtured in return

(3) how you nurture yourself.

Not many people are good at nurturing others or themselves but enjoy someone nurturing them. The Moon tells us a lot about nurturing and how you experience it.

Venus is connections. It has a plus sign sitting under a circle and this plus sign draws and connects you to others, it is the network planet. Look for the sign Venus is in, its house and what planets are in aspect to it, particularly conjunct or opposite. Venus tells us about how you relate, how friendly you are, supportive, pleasant, rude, generous or selfish. Are you demanding in friendship? Are you generous with your love and affection? Look at most of Venus' key words, they aren't exclusively about love, they are particularly focused on 'attraction' and 'connection'.

You have the Moon as the nurturer, Venus as social attraction and connection but where is true love? Where is your soul's partner? Ah ha, that is found in the rest of the chart and that is where a professional astrologer examines to locate and delineate specific details about your love life.

I have yet to mention the role of the 7th house which is very important in providing more clues to love, marriage and partners in your chart. To better understand the 7th house let me tell you about **Romantic Love**. Romantic Love is said to be composed of three legs, like a stool – passion, intimacy and commitment.

A three legged stool is most stable when all three legs are firmly placed on the ground. Remove one leg and the stool is at risk of collapsing.

The first leg is **Passion.** Consider how sexual attraction, passion, is very much like a match: you strike it and it flares brightly for a few seconds. The match then slowly burns to finally turn into ash. A love affair is much like the match stick, it flares brightly, continues to burn while there's fuel (affection, romance, lust, youth, physical beauty). Once it runs out of fuel the flame is extinguished. Romantic love needs passion and passion needs fuel. Candlelit dinners, a weekend away from the children, sexual time together, these are powerful fuels that can keep the flame of passion alive in a relationship.

The 2nd leg of the stool is **Intimacy**. Intimacy is best described as the quiet moments lovers spend together sharing their desires, interests, fears and grand visions. New lovers spend a lot of time getting to know each other intimately. Intimacy is vital in keeping romantic love alive in your relationship.

The 3rd leg is **Commitment**. Commitment describes a long term relationship in which the partners stay together because they have committed to the relationship for one of many reasons. It could be financial; it could be that affection and intimacy have remained strong over time; it could be for the children; it could be for companionship; it might be the fear of being alone; and it could be because they have nowhere else to go.

A relationship generally begins with passion, it starts with great intensity, like a bright, burning flame. Things eventually settles down as intimacy is gained during those passionate moments which help bind the couple together. Finally, as the passion fades and intimacy turns to boredom or disinterest, commitment can become the leg that holds the stool upright. This becomes the glue which holds the couple together.

It is an interesting theory and one that you might consider in your professional counselling and astrology work.

Most people think that passion is love, but passion is just one factor that forms the construct of love. As you age your understanding of love will shift. Where once passion was the centre stone, over time it can die off to be replaced by intimacy and then finally commitment. If you are lucky your three legged stool will keep all three legs strong and robust in the face of adversity. Romantic love takes time and effort, it really is hard work, just ask anyone who has endured a long-term relationship.

So what, you ask, does this have to do with the 7th house? The 7th house describes the type of person you are attracted to, and the type of person whom you attract in turn. The sign on its cusp and any planets inside the 7th will also tell you about these three factors: your strength of Passion, your level of Intimacy and your ability to remain Committed.

The 7th house also tells you about your level of tolerance and desire for passion, intimacy and commitment. When reading a chart these three qualities can inform your client of what to expect from themselves and from their partner. Combining these three elements may help them make wise decisions in love.

Your astrology chart, of course, contains information on all facets of Romantic Love, not just passion, intimacy or of commitment. Have you worked out which combinations of planets, signs or houses best describe each leg of your own construct of Romantic Love? Have a look at your Moon and Venus signs, planetary aspects and house placements. Next, determine what is happening with the sign on your 7th cusp and examine the planets, if any, residing in your 7th house? These are your personal guides who will help you understand how to gain a fulfilling, romantic relationship in your life.

Chapter 8 - The Aries Myth and the Spring Equinox

On the 21st March the Sun reaches the equator on its journey north thus signalling the start of Spring in the northern hemisphere. This is the exact moment the Sun enters the sign of Aries and is called the Spring or Vernal Equinox. Here in the southern hemisphere it is the Autumnal Equinox.

With the arrival of Spring you can see new-born lambs frolicking in the fields and a multitude of gorgeous flowers clamouring to attract bees to pollinate the next generation. It is a time to celebrate the fertility of the fields.

In countries where Winter is particularly harsh, visitors delightedly join in with the locals in their Spring celebrations. The saying, 'as mad as a March hare', is still used today to describe people's exuberance at the start of Spring. In ancient times the Roman Spring festival of Kalends was an opportunity to party, spend freely and to give generously. Even today we evoke ancient myths to welcome the pleasant weather of Spring after the cold grip of Winter.

In the Mithraic religion followers celebrated the death and rebirth of the God Mithrais at the Spring Equinox. This religion appears to have formed the foundations for some of the traditions and beliefs of Christianity. Mithraism was the popular choice of religion of the Roman military. To this day much of the Mithraic religion remains shrouded in secrecy as followers were not permitted to record their rituals.

The Venerable Bede, a British monk of the 8th century, wrote that Christianity had borrowed the pagan festival of Eastra (Eostre), the Saxon Goddess of Spring, and called it 'Easter' to celebrate Christ's death and rebirth. The only reference we have to this Goddess is his commentary: *"Eosturmononath has a name which is now translated as 'Paschal month,' and which was once called after a goddess of theirs named Eostre, in whose honor feasts were celebrated in that month. Now they designate the Paschal season by her name, calling the joys of the new rite by the time-honoured name of the old observance."* (De Temporum Ratione, 725 AD).

Eastra may be Ishtar, the Babylonian and Assyrian goddess of love and fertility. The names of the two Goddesses are similar in pronunciation but unfortunately we do not have enough information on Eastra to know if they are one and the same. The Easter Bunny's gift of chocolate rabbits and eggs on Easter Sunday is most likely connected with the Eastra pagan fertility celebrations.

During the 17th and 18th century many American Puritans and Protestants considered Easter (and Christmas) as far too 'pagan' for them to celebrate. They complained that it was simply an excuse for revellers to party, drink and engage in lascivious behaviour.

The most celebrated Greek Goddess attributed to Spring is Persephone, the daughter of Demeter (her Roman name is Ceres) and Zeus (his Roman name is Jupiter/Jove). This is her myth: Hades (his Roman name is Pluto), the God of the Underworld, fell in love with Persephone. In an act of desperation he drove his chariot out of his underworld kingdom and kidnapped the young and beautiful Persephone. When her mother, Demeter, discovered what had happened she petitioned Zeus to force Hades to release her daughter.

Alas, Persephone had eaten a seed while in the Underworld thus condemning her to remain with Hades as his wife. Hearing this news, Demeter, the Goddess of fertility, withdrew her blessing from the people of the earth. Their crops failed, people starved and everyone blamed Zeus. Zeus succumbed to the people's outrage and permitted Persephone to live with her mother from Spring to Autumn. Persephone and Demeter, rulers of fertility and agriculture, also presided over the Eleusinian Mysteries of the cult of Demeter which promised the believer a joyful and fruitful afterlife.

In examining the myth of Aries we can see how the ancients would consider Winter as a form of death. Spring arose in all its glory as confirmation of the renewal of life. The modern celebration of Easter evokes similar themes: death and rebirth. It is an allegorical triumph of light over darkness, of good over evil. This theme also parallels the hero's journey which forms the foundations of the Fire element - Aries, Leo and Sagittarius.

The ancient Babylonians celebrated the Spring Equinox by recognising the importance of agriculture and in particular, the farm worker. The image of the ram came later with the Persians and Egyptians who saw him as a symbol of fertility.

The zodiac sign of Aries is represented by the ram, the virile male sheep. In the rutting season he bursts with an abundance of libido and vigour to inseminate his flock of up to fifty ewes. It is during this period that he is aggressive and preoccupied in securing and servicing his ewes. He can become so fixated in fighting off competitors that he will often forget to mate with his ewes and even to eat.

Any sheep farmer will tell you: never let children enter a paddock or enclosure if there is a ram present. Rams have a reputation for butting, often causing severe injuries and sometimes death. Rams have been known to fight each other until one or the other is injured, some die.

Rams are inherently predisposed to assume a position of dominance, humans are therefore considered subservient to them, particularly if ewes are present. Rams will interpret a touch, push or tickle of their head as a challenge to fight. Farmers will warn anyone entering a paddock containing a ram to continually note its location while they work. A ram can butt without warning or provocation.

Like an Aries child, rams are boisterous and impulsive, but they can be trained, or, more correctly, they can be 'socialised'. We do this with our puppies by sending them to 'puppy school' and then giving them access to other dogs in supervised play areas. Socialisation is an important part in training a headstrong Aries to get along with others.

Why did our ancestors assign the ram to the constellation of Aries? Was it his impulsive, aggressive and single-minded nature that they had in mind? Although I agree with the image of a virile, libidinal ram as their preferred option, I can't help but wonder why they didn't chose a flower or a bee. Why didn't they choose something that more closely represents the obvious fertility of Spring? Perhaps it is the blast of vitality that Spring brings that swayed them to choose the ram.

I often need to remind myself that the ancients lived closer to nature than we do today. Many would have been farmers and many would have had direct personal contact with their animals, particularly herd animals like sheep.

It is believed that sheep were the first animals tamed by humans. They are placid, smallish herd animals and their behaviour is quite simple: they will follow a leader. A flock of sheep will follow their shepherd because they know he will protect them and lead them to water and sweet grasses. The shepherd becomes their leader.

The myth of Aries has been passed down to us from the ancient Greeks, immortalised in the legend of 'Jason and the Argonauts' and his quest for the Golden Fleece.

The myth goes like this: Hermes was asked by Zeus to send Aries, the magical flying ram with the golden fleece, to rescue the son and daughter of Athamas, the King of Boeotia. Aries carried Phrixus and his sister Helle on his back to escape their vengeful step-mother. The Hellespont (today named the Dardanelles), the body of water that bridges the Black Sea with the Aegean Sea, is named in honour of Helle.

To celebrate his successful escape to the city of Colchis, on the far eastern coast of the Black Sea, Phrixus sacrificed the ram and gave the golden fleece to his protector, King Aeetes. Aeetes hung Aries golden fleece in a sacred grove guarded by a fierce dragon. When Jason (Jason and the Argonauts) learned of such a treasure he set out on his quest to steal this magical golden fleece and lay claim to his own kingdom - and so a legend is born.

As reward for his brave act in rescuing the children, Zeus placed Aries in the night sky as the constellation of Aries.

It is important not to get Aries the Ram confused with Ares the God of War - please note the subtle difference in spelling. Ares was the son of Zeus and Hera, he wasn't too bright but he did love to fight. His sister, Athena, was the Goddess of War but was far more strategic than her rash brother. Bloodthirsty Ares had few friends but what he did have was the bed of Aphrodite. The Roman God of War, Mars, is the Greek Ares.

This article by Noel Eastwood, appeared in the **Federation of Australian Astrologers** March 2019 Journal – Vol.49, No. 1

Chapter 9 - Psychology, the brain and EEG biofeedback

I would like to tell you about one part of my practice that I find simply fascinating, and that is how the brain can be trained through EEG biofeedback, which is also known as Neurofeedback. EEG is short for electroencephalograph, it is the instrument that reads or measures brainwaves.

My psychotherapy studies taught me that personality problems in later life were the result of childhood trauma, this is very Freudian. In university I was taught that all behaviour was learned and this is very much Skinner's Behaviourism. Of course, both are valid in their own way. However, after studying and practising biofeedback and neurofeedback, I've grown in my understanding of the brain's enormous role in psychopathology.

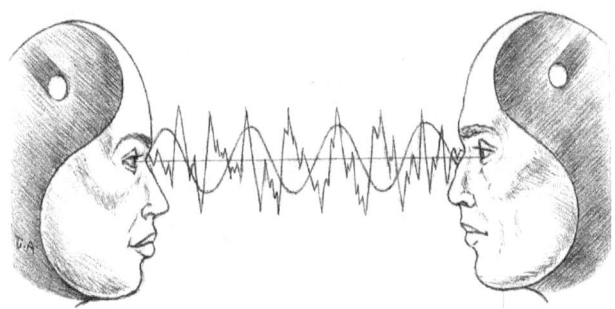

The brain is composed of two halves, they look the same but their function is quite different. The vast majority of humans, and other mammals, are right handed. For these people the left hemisphere is known as the 'dominant' hemisphere. This is where we process language, therefore it must run fast, very fast, in the frequencies between 15 and 20 Hertz (Hz).

From my experience and that of other neurofeedback practitioners, about half of all left handed people also have a dominant left hemisphere. The other left handed people are true left handers therefore their dominant hemisphere is on the right. That means that they process language in the right hemisphere. For the rest of this chapter I will only refer to right handed people.

The left hemisphere contains special sites for attending to human speech. The sound of a human voice is detected and processed for content and meaning in these sites.

The brain will always attend to the sounds of a human voice. The right hemisphere listens for its emotional content while the left hemisphere listens for its meaning.

> the sound of a human voice can indicate the threat of danger or of pleasure (enemy or friend),

> the language centre in the left Temporal Lobe immediately recognises the vocalisations as words,

> this information goes to the left Parietal Lobe where the sounds are interpreted (decoded) for meaning,

> the decoded message is then sent to the left Frontal Lobe where a suitable response is formed and delivered.

All this is done in the blink of an eye, therefore very fast brainwaves are needed to do that.

The right hemisphere has no language centres, its hearing centre only listens for environmental sounds. What this means is that it listens for the context of its environment such as a lion roaring, a car screeching, the sounds of the wind in a tree or a stone axe clinking against a rock. It will also register the sound of a human scream of fear or anger triggering an immediate survival response.

When the right hemisphere registers human voices it interprets for emotion and searches for context that allows the brain to form a picture of the person who is speaking. It doesn't register WHAT they are saying but HOW they are saying it. This is primarily a survival reflex, "*am I safe with this person?*"

If the sounds are emotion-driven it will trigger a '*flight - fight - freeze*' response. The right hemisphere will immediately engage the Limbic, or emotional system, via the right Amygdula so that they can immediately react. If the sounds are of a predator we run; if the sounds suggest it is an enemy we run; if the sounds suggest it is a friend we will approach and feel warm inside.

The right hemisphere prefers slow brainwave frequencies in the sleep to relaxed-alert ranges, 0-15 Hz. These are from the Delta, Theta, Alpha and Sensory Motor Rhythm (SMR).

The left hemisphere registers a human voice and decodes for meaning, while the right hemisphere decodes for safety and builds the bigger picture of what type of person is speaking. The Frontal Lobes are then enabled to form a suitable response.

Thus we have one brain, but each half of that brain acts separately, for many different reasons.

We know from Attachment Theory that the right hemisphere is where most of our psychological issues arise such as anxiety, racing negative thoughts, and even hyperactivity.

When the right hemisphere is relaxed it runs very slowly, in the sleep frequencies. When stressed it runs super fast, in the beta frequencies - above 15 Hz which is like 'red-lining' a racing car - way too fast for the right brain to remain comfortable and stable. This increase in frequency creates anxiety.

Anxiety is a normal reaction to a stimuli that requires arousal of the physical and mental body. We jump up and fight or we run away. Sometimes, when the right Amygdula and right orbito-frontal cortex are continually over-stimulated, we might even just freeze. This happens in children who are witness to continued domestic violence. This is also seen in adults who have a history of abuse.

Stress damages the brain: both hemispheres are effected by stress hormones which should only be in the blood stream for a short period of time.

Millions of years ago when our ancestors were small, upright hominids learning to survive in the grasslands of central and east Africa, they would experience elevated levels of stress when confronted by danger. This would cause them to quickly run to safety. Because of their small Frontal Lobes these prehumans would soon forget what they were stressed about. The stress hormones in their bloodstream would drop off quickly as they sat high and safe in their tree. They might watch a butterfly or eat a juicy grub and soon forget that they were stressed only moments earlier.

Modern humans are sensitive, they have large Frontal Lobes which can stay stressed for days, weeks and even years. Stress hormones will then remain in the blood stream to oxidise into neurotoxins which damages the nerves of the central nervous system (CNS or brain).

How do stress hormones impact on your personality? Your right Amygdula triggers an adrenal response (Adrenaline) when you are stressed. Symptoms include: anxiety, panic attacks, forgetfulness, memory lapses, flat mood/depression, physical nervousness and agitation, hyperactivity and hyper vigilance. There are dozens more symptoms but I think you get the picture. It doesn't need to experience anything directly, just thinking about something stressful will set off the production of Adrenaline.

The right hemisphere can be trained to slow down to its usual 0-15 Hz with enough training be it meditation, processing and problem solving, goal setting, counselling, psychotherapy, talking to a trusted friend, exercise, or EEG biofeedback / neurofeedback. For some individuals this will even eliminate their symptoms. Yes, EEG biofeedback (neurofeedback) really does work but it takes an experienced therapist and many training sessions to retrain the brain. Not everyone will respond but it is a very useful tool for psychologists.

If you think EEG biofeedback/neurofeedback would be useful for you or someone you know, please do a search for therapists in your local area.

Chapter 10 - The mystics path – 1

Sometimes I see people who seek to walk the path least travelled, the mystics path. I say 'least travelled' because it really is. Many talk about it, many write about it but so few really walk it.

The mystics path requires exceptional dedication, daily meditations using specific meditation forms. The path is lonely, incredibly lonely. Who do these students of life talk to as they experience the wonders of walking their inner world? Who understands the extreme personal sacrifices needed to take this journey within?

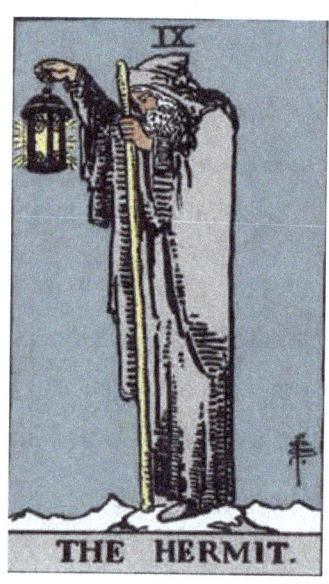

The mystic's path is known in every religion and spiritual pursuit. I have had the honour of working intimately with Christian, Muslim, Hindu, pagan, atheists, Buddhists, Taoists and just ordinary people seeking to *know thyself*. Interestingly it is much the same experience for each: external service and activity is balanced by the inner journey.

Many years ago I worked with a woman who gave of herself, as a Christian is taught is Christ's way, but her giving only increased her Christian friends taking from her. These friends used her generosity of spirit for their own gain. When she was in need they were not there for her. This eventually pitched her into the depths of depression.

We talked about her beliefs and I decided to introduce her to the mystics path, for her it was the Christian mystic path. When I mentioned my thoughts she became very interested, this was a completely new concept for her. I explained that the mystics path was not for the fainthearted, it took deliberate, dedicated practice and devotion to walk the path, to *know thyself.*

This gentle lady slowly shifted from hours of debilitating depression and mind-numbing anxiety to one of inner peace. She dedicated herself to practising her daily meditations, breathing exercises and specific mental imagery.

I chose to introduce her to the mystics path primarily because I saw something special in her. She had a deep and profound faith in her religious beliefs. I saw that she had the foundations on which to heal herself at a soul level, and that must always come from within.

Her other options weren't very positive. I could have chosen other useful psychotherapy techniques but her devotion to her faith was strong, very strong. This was what the path requires, dedication to a purpose and the self discipline to continue along that path.

She was already meditating with her 'inner selves' by this time so I decided to shift things towards the mystics path and took her inside Pluto's Cave which I consider to be the portal to the unconscious.

I introduced her to her inner world represented by a cave complete with a comfy bed, a kitchen, fireplace, study desk and even a bathroom. Outside the cave entrance was a grassy lawn overlooking a lagoon and snow capped mountains in the distance.

A cave is a useful metaphor for going within your unconscious. A cave is also representative of the 8th and 12th houses which some believe represent endings and beginnings. A cave can be a resting place to withdraw from the world. It represents safety and sanctuary like the womb from which we all came. For the purposes of therapy I consider Pluto's Cave, any cave, as the portal to the underworld, and that is the unconscious.

I'm sure not everyone likes caves. If this lady didn't like the cave imagery I would simply shift to something more suitable, perhaps a garden, a cottage on the beach or maybe a farm house. One of my patients, severely abused as a child, was most comfortable in her garden with her pets, some farm animals, friends and selected family members there to support her. An inner sanctuary is a place you can go when healing is needed, deep healing.

As an astrologer I like to travel within to meet my astrology archetypes, they act as my inner guides. I frequently use the Sun and Moon archetypes. At other times I will draw a tarot card which becomes my inner guide for that specific meditation. Archetypal meditations are incredibly powerful guides or entryways into the unconscious.

The mystic's meditations lay the foundations necessary to shift into emotional healing, astral travel and other fascinating experiences that come by walking the mystics path.

I wanted to discuss the mystics path because it most certainly is the least travelled and least understood. I enjoy working with people walking this path, they appreciate that it takes time and effort and that it can be very lonely at times.

If you are walking this path please ensure that you have emotional support and a comfortable place to practice. Don't be put off by life, keep coming back to your daily practices. My words to you are: don't stop, keep doing, but go slowly, gently and don't give up.

Chapter 11 - The mystics path - 2

There are some interesting astrological pointers that may help you on your mystics path. Mystics have certain personal qualities that can be seen in the chart if you know what to look for.

How is a mystic different to other people? It is quite simple: they practice attaining a state of quiet and internal silence generally through meditation; they exercise both physically and mentally; and their habits and behaviours are dedicated to the achievement of enlightenment. The mystic knows that enlightenment is a journey and not a destination. If they don't achieve enlightenment in this lifetime they are quite comfortable and prepared to come back and try again in the next.

I know that a lot of people practice meditation yet they are not mystics nor are they on the path. So becoming a mystic can not simply be dedication to the daily practice of meditation. So what could it be?

I have looked at many a mystic's astrology chart and there is sometimes very little to remark about their astrological makeup. In fact what you would expect to be strong in a mystic's chart is not always what makes them different.

What I have discovered is that the mystic has been challenged by life and for many reasons has come through stronger and with qualities that others have abandoned in their struggles.

Some people think that a mystic is magical, that they have special psychic powers and an enlightened understanding of the universe. However exciting and appealing this may be it is not the case. A mystic is a warrior of the spirit, someone who seeks to understand the meaning of life which may not always be through occult practices.

A scientist, a monk or nun, a plumber or a mathematician, a house wife, a warehouse worker, an unemployed misfit, a student of law or a humble labourer can walk this path least travelled. It is their dedication to a purpose with the qualities of self discipline, humility, kindness and compassion.

A company director with psychopathic traits commanding billions of dollars can also have many of these qualities. What they do not have is empathy and compassion for others. The higher purpose that a mystic seeks to immerse in is absent in the psychopath. Where the psychopath attends to his/her bank balance and the satisfaction of their impulsive urges the mystic attends to their most basic needs rather than their basic urges.

I do need to make it clear that the mystic does not gamble with charity, charity always begins at home. With most charities these days delivering roughly 20% of donations to their actual cause it is no wonder the mystic chooses to give directly and not via the charity or church. The mystic gives wisely and responsibly and rarely does this involve money.

Often a Fire chart shows stronger intuition than Water charts which are traditionally accepted as the psychic element. Water dominated people can often have psychic impressions but lack accurate insight normally attributed to them.

A key feature is groundedness which is the most important Earth element quality. Another is intuition, creativity and psychic energy of the Fire dominated person. A third quality is the Water dominated person's sensitivity, empathy and compassion. The last is Air which brings intellect and the ability to sift through illusion and denial to gain clarity and understanding.

What is quite clear is that you need ALL of the elements: Earth, Air, Water and Fire. The more balanced the elements are the easier it is for the mystic to walk along their path.

Two elements that stand out though are Fire and Water. You can see this in any number of formations, constellations and signatures in the astrology chart. Too much of one element puts them out of balance though. For instance, too much Fire leads to hyperactivity, narcissism and selfishness rather than creativity, intuition and inspiration. Too much Water leads to feelings of loneliness, abandonment and betrayal rather than insight, empathy, awareness and sensitivity.

But having plenty of Fire and Water is useless if there isn't any Earth to ground it. You need to have the dedication, self discipline and determination to practice your meditations, and some of those exercises are not easy.

Finally you need Air. You need intellectual clarity to cut through the illusions of the imagination and the clouding nature of denial. It is no good having fun in the astral plane if you lack the intelligence to process what to do with this insight.

Are there specific constellations in the astrology chart that shows someone is a mystic? No, however I look for planetary aspects that show hardship, squares and oppositions. These tell me that this person has had to confront the challenges of life, that they have had to learn how to moderate their basic instincts and urges to overcome them.

I also look for conjunctions between an outer planet (Jupiter, Chiron, Saturn, Uranus, Neptune or Pluto) and one of the luminaries (Sun or Moon). This highlights the source of their personal power. Each outer planet has power of specific form that can be accessed through these conjunctions. A mystic learns how to tap into these powers and thus earn the right to use them.

Finally I look for a balance of elements, though not always obvious as you will need to look at house cusps, rulerships and sign dominance. A lack of an element however can be of similar use as the conjunction between a luminary and a powerful outer planet. The mystic learns how to access the specific power of that missing element. In other words a professional astrologer looks at the chart as a whole and not for a single indicator.

Can you walk the mystics path? I am certain anyone can but be warned that it takes mentorship, depth psychoanalysis (which you can learn to do yourself), specific forms of meditation and then you must stick with it.

Chapter 12 - Bringing back the dead

I was watching an episode of *Through The Wormhole* on TV when they said that they would present a show on bringing back the dead... but, I thought to myself, why? Why bring back the dead? And what is so special about zombies anyway, isn't that what they'll end up as?

We still can't identify consciousness, we can't even agree on what consciousness is. Besides, if we did isolate consciousness we have no way of storing it let alone being able to transfer it from one being to another. I really don't know if we will ever be able to do that.

Why are we so interested in doing this? What is it with this fascination we have for zombies?

What if you could go to the other side of consciousness though, to death itself, and experienced that instead? Would you then want to be brought back to life after you have died?

Just now I was thinking, '*but we do recycle, we do come back from death, we reincarnate*'. But this chapter isn't going to be about past lives, though that is on my list, it is about how we might be able to explore what is beyond our current level of consciousness.

I have always given this considerable thought but then I do have six planets in the 8th house and most of them conjunct Pluto. Maybe that is why I dwell on the inner world so much.

Can the average person enter a state where they can touch upon the dimensions beyond consciousness? A world within all of us, to enter Pluto's Cave, the underworld of myth and legend?

Is there some simple technique or method that you can use to enter your personal underworld where you can access this source of creation, the actual mechanism that creates your existence?

Well, yes, there are many techniques to go beyond, and apart from drugs, they all start with relaxation. It is such a simple way to separate from the 'here and now'.

The practice of relaxation, and I mean a deep progressive relaxation, helps you detach from your surroundings and to go within, within your unconscious. Simple? Yes, it really can be that simple. When you close your eyes, within a half second, your brain begins to reduce fast Beta brainwaves (15 to 40 Hertz). As your brain slows it begins to produce strong Alpha brainwaves (8 to 12 Hertz). This puts you into a calm, empty-minded state where there are no thoughts. It is a prelude to falling asleep.

Alpha is the state you go into when looking out of the window to stare into the distance. No thoughts, just *'off with the fairies'*. Alpha is called 'the resting state of the brain'.

Alpha is very important to your mental health and the health of your Central Nervous System (CNS). Relaxing, going for walks, and even looking into the distance, are ways to calm your mind. It calms those racing thoughts to allow it to slow and eventually settle. It is nature's way of giving your busy mind a break.

Alpha is the state that drug addicts, alcoholics and marijuana users enjoy. Unfortunately they generally develop a tolerance to their drug and have difficulty producing enough alpha to relax and especially to fall asleep. They then need to use more drugs or alcohol to relax.

If you continue with your relaxation, eyes closed, breath slowing and deepening, just slightly, your brainwaves shift down another gear, down into Theta. The Theta State (4 to 8 Hertz) is also called the Lucid or Dream State. In the Theta State you have just lost consciousness and you are starting to dream creating lucid images and flashes of insight. Your thought processes start to slow even more and you now have access to your unconscious.

This is the state that hypnotherapists use to access memories. It is where you can program your mind to do amazing things.

With your breath you have a technique to take you into your unconscious. It is simple because you breathe every day. You fall asleep and pass through this lucid state at least twice each night, going into sleep and waking up.

But there are some techniques that you can use to speed up the process of entering your personal inner world. These techniques are a means to relax faster and deeper in preparation for lucid dreaming. Remote viewing, astral travel and out of body travel are just a few experiences that you can develop in this state.

One exercise I teach is the practice of slow deep breathing: breath in for 5 seconds and out for 5 seconds. This is called Heart Rate Variability training which replicates the heart-lung coherence. Your heart will beat slightly faster as you breathe in, and then it beats slightly slower as you breathe out. Why? Because when your lungs fill with air your heart is forced into a smaller area within your chest cavity. It is squeezed slightly causing it to beat just a little faster and a little harder. On the out breath the pressure on your heart eases and it relaxes allowing it to beat a little slower. When both the heart and lung coordinate their activity it is called 'heart-lung coherence'.

Most Westerners have lost this 'coherence' from lack of exercise and shallow breathing. Their heart sometimes beats out of rhythm with what their lungs are doing.

This technique is simply applying a 10 second breath cycle - 5 seconds in and 5 seconds out. This is also used for Heart Rate Variability biofeedback training. This form of biofeedback uses a pulse measuring device which is clipped to your finger, like those used in hospitals.

The 10 second breath cycle is recognised as perhaps the best breathing technique for improving your health. You can incorporate this breathing cycle to improve your ability to relax too. Ten minutes of deliberate deep breathing will improve your life and your sleep will improve as well.

One elderly fellow I worked with was always depressed and I mean ALWAYS. His wife of fifty years explained that this was such a burden on their family. One day I decided to measure his Oxygen levels using a finger clip pulse monitor. His SpO2 was 93% which is considered below normal, it should be higher (above 95%). I suggested that he perform the Heart Rate Variability breathing technique for ten minutes in our session. It was tiring for him, five seconds in and five seconds out wouldn't normally upset anyone but when you are unhealthy and unwell it can be a struggle. He was quite unfit and I had to keep reminding him to breathe. When I saw him a few days later he was buoyant, he said he had never slept so well in years.

Chapter 13 - Life after death

My father told us kids of how he died when he was 15 years old. His appendix had burst during an emergency operation to remove it. He said that all of a sudden he found himself at the Pearly Gates of Heaven. As he walked up to the gates Saint Peter held his hand up and stopped him from entering.

"Hold on sonny, you can't go in there without your ticket," announced Saint Peter.

So my father looked in his pockets but couldn't find his 'ticket to heaven'.

Saint Peter shrugged and said, *"In that case you need to go back to where you came from."*

I've had a few clients tell me of their death experiences, interestingly most died on the operating table. They all said the same thing: they could see and hear everything that was going on in the operating theatre. They felt themselves hovering above or near their body and could clearly hear each word spoken and saw all that went on as they were revived.

One man was operated on while lying on his side and covered with a sheet. He physically could not have seen anything even if he had wanted to. When his heart stopped beating he felt himself lift above his body and float to just below the ceiling of the operating room.

In a detached manner he saw the nurses and the doctors in a panic trying to revive him. The next day when he had recovered enough to speak he told one of the nurses that he had seen and heard everything in the operating room while he was revived. He even relayed the panicked cry from the emergency doctor:

"He'll die right now if we don't get this bloody piece of s__t machine to work!"

I remember how he told me that the nurse he spoke to went as white as a ghost when he told her.

Not many people progress much further than the moment of death and revival. One woman saw Jesus who told her that she wasn't meant to stay with him just yet. He said she had things to do before she could come back to be with him. That was a life changing moment for her and invigorated her desire to live a meaningful life.

Most survivors never say a thing to their medical staff, not even to their family or partners, for fear of being accused of lying or being just plain crazy. Fortunately they sometimes tell me. Because I have been-there-done-that with my own out of body experiences I have been able to help normalise theirs.

Does life continue after death? I believe so. Some of the people I have spoken to said that it was initially frightening but they became quickly accustomed to floating above their body. They felt strangely aloof, detached yet fascinated by what they saw going on around them. They each told me that it was a wonderful experience which words fail to adequately describe.

Sadly, many people enjoy humiliating those who speak of their near-death experiences and so it remains in that grey area of fringe psychology and medicine. Just as sadly, some of those who failed to experience these magical moments become sceptics, taking pleasure in denigrating those who have. No wonder so many survivors don't say a thing.

Chapter 14 – Excerpt: The Fool's Journey through the Tarot Pentacles

The **Fool's Journey series** by Noel Eastwood

The Ace of Pentacles

Embarking on an earthly adventure.

Eve returned home just as the sun was setting. On the back porch she strung up the herbs she had gathered that day and took off her cloak and heavy, mud spattered boots.

"Follin, I'm home," she called out as she did each evening to an empty silence. As she went inside she noticed that the cottage was warm and that the banked fire in the grate still glowed. *'Must be this new wood,'* she thought. She stoked the fire and swung the kettle over it. The candle on the table needed replacing so she went to the cupboard in the hall. As she lit her candle, Eve heard a soft sound coming from her bedroom. *'Next door's cat asleep on my bed again,'* she thought.

"Come on, time to go home," Eve said as she entered the bedroom to shoo him off.

"But I am home," said a sleepy voice from the bed.

Eve wiped away her tears as she lay the flower wreath on her little sister's grave. It was this final act that cemented her conviction to leave behind the remains of her past and set out on her own journey. It felt like the end of life but, in reality, it was the beginning, sparked by her first meeting with Follin, some years earlier.

They had met at the crossroads on the outskirts of her village. He had looked so lost and confused that Eve had no choice but to feel sorry for this handsome, yet fragile, young man. The memory of sitting in the grass together, sharing her lunch and talking of life and the future, had remained with her.

At that time there was a wary peace in the Mystic Isle. She lived with her parents in the village and when her parents were away from home, Eve and her little sister, Gabriela, would stay with their grandparents in the forest. Things were simple then, life held few complications and she was happy.

She and Follin were both just kids, barely out of puberty, when they had first met. The spark that ignited at the moment of their meeting had continued to burn.

Eve often returned to the place where they had met: a grassy glade beside the forest track near her grandparents' house.

"Oh, Follin, where are you now? I need you so much," she would sigh, sitting alone in the grass, twirling a golden dandelion flower, staring into space.

It was there, sitting in the grass, that she had recalled Follin saying he lived on the edge of the deep forest in the south of the Mystic Isle. It was a small village, right on the edge of the island. She was an Isle girl herself. Her home was in the far north-east, where the Wildlanders often landed to make raids on the villages. Eve had joked that they both were half Wildlander and half Mystic Islander, harbouring wild magic of all the elements.

Follin had told her that he was on a journey to find his father, or, perhaps, it was to find himself. Eve saw that he did not know where he was heading. He had mentioned some of the people he had met on his journey and told her of some of his adventures. She had sat entranced as he spoke - his was a true adventure of the spirit that she now yearned for.

Eve recalled him telling her about his brother who had died from the plague, brought by invaders some years earlier. This crippled his father who had fought to prevent the sickness ravaging his beloved isle, but he could not prevent it ravaging his own family. The shy young man had then described how his family struggled to survive after his father abandoned them - a broken man.

Follin had told her that his father was a mage, well known in the Mystic Isle and in the outer kingdoms – even the Wildlands. But he was powerless to save his own son. No longer able to live with himself, his father disappeared, to where no one knew. In some ways Follin's own journey was to understand his father, to find his father's legacy within himself.

The Lovers had met just the once, some years ago. Where Follin went next, she had no idea. All she could think of was to find him, not that it made any sense, she thought. She remembered the name of his village, *Saoirse*. Follin had explained that it meant *be true to yourself,* and that was what he was seeking on his journey – his true self.

Soon after her meeting with Follin the north was invaded. Eve's father and mother were taken to serve in the army and died shortly afterward. She had tried to make ends meet for herself and her little sister but the war made it almost impossible to survive. After the invaders had pillaged and plundered the countryside the islanders began to starve.

Her once friendly neighbours became competitors for food and resources - if they could gain an advantage over another to feed their families, they would. To Eve's horror, she saw loyal islanders betray their friends for security and food from the enemy soldiers. She witnessed neighbours who had once invited their friends to break bread at their table now readily betray them to survive. The world she thought she knew was gone, replaced by a violent, bitter world where friends became enemies.

Eve had tried to help where she could. She had learned enough healing from her grandparents and parents to be of use to the community. It was one way she could earn enough to feed herself and her little sister. But her knowledge and skill in healing was not enough when disease soon followed starvation. The invasion had laid waste to everything she knew and loved.

In that final act of laying flowers on Gabriela's grave, Eve realised that finding Follin was her last reason to stay alive.

"So that's when you came looking for me?" asked Follin, his eyes red from his tears as she related her story.

"Yes. I remembered the name of your village and the directions you gave me. That's how I found my way here." It was still too early to get out of bed so they lay together, cherishing the warmth of their naked bodies against each other.

"I'm so sorry, Eve. If I had known what you were destined to experience I would have come looking for you earlier." He pulled her closer then kissed her wet cheeks.

Follin had just arrived from his sojourn in the Tarot Empire with the Major Arcana, this was only their second morning together. There was so much to catch up on since their first meeting almost four years ago.

"You don't know where your mother and sister went either, do you, Follin?" Eve leaned on one elbow to look at him. She recognised that her lover had also lost so much while he was away.

"No, I don't know where they are. My father left when I was about ten, since then all I've known is hardship. I blamed myself for his leaving, but I now know that he had his own demons to conquer."

Follin sniffed back tears threatening to flood his eyes. "I've seen his childhood, and the horrors he lived through, in my meditations. The fighting, witnessing his own family taken... what is it about humans that we do such terrible things to each other?"

Eve pulled her hand from the warm covers and placed it on his cheek. She followed the path of tears from his eyes to his throat then kissed him again.

"My love, it seems we are destined to repeat the same horrors year after year, lifetime after lifetime. The day they took my parents to serve in the war I was staying with my grandparents in the mountains. When I arrived home, Gabriela came out of hiding and told me what had happened. They were such good people, they didn't deserve to be taken away from us." Eve stopped to look up at the thatched ceiling. She watched several mice run along the beams above. They had been her daily companions since she had arrived there. Seeing them always gave her comfort.

"We lost nearly all the food in our larder, and the chickens, they were all taken by our own soldiers. Then the enemy soldiers came and took the last of what we'd hidden. It was at night, we could see the fires in the distance. They burnt my village. I took Gabriela to hide in the forest where we lived on herbs, mushrooms and roots. When the soldiers had gone we came back to find almost everyone dead and our house burned to the ground. Later I heard a rumour that my grandparents had fled but no one knew where."

"How did you survive?" Follin could feel her heart beating against his chest.

Eve smiled when she remembered her little sister, how brave Gabriela was, but then her face clouded over as she continued the story. "The soldiers left their dead behind and the smell of all those bodies was horrible. We went through their clothing looking for food. We found some stale bread, barely enough to last for a few days. Then Gabriela became sick. The soldiers had brought the plague with them and left it behind for us. Our neighbours who had hidden in the forest with us died, too. I was the only one who didn't get sick. I don't know why I was saved, but I was left alive when I should have died. I wanted to die. I was so scared and so alone." She turned and stared into Follin's bright eyes. "You know what saved me?" she asked.

Follin shook his head.

"You," she said.

"What? Me? But I wasn't there," he said, surprised.

"All I could think of was being with you. That's what kept me going, that's what kept me alive. I searched and searched until I found your village. I asked the gatekeeper where you lived and he warned me that your family had long gone and the house was falling apart. I wasn't afraid, I knew you would find me." Eve dropped her head back onto the pillow.

"I had dreams of being with you, Eve. I saw you asleep on this bed, in my arms, just like now. I saw it so many times it felt real," he told her.

Follin felt Eve withdraw from him.

"Follin," Eve said in a quiet voice. "There's something else I need to tell you."

'Yes?" he said and waited. Eve was silent. Follin drew her back to him and kissed her forehead. "What is it, my love?"

"You need to know that I told the gatekeeper that I am your wife. I thought the villagers would not let me live here otherwise. I told them that we were married in my village up north, that then we were separated and you had told me to come here and wait for you."

"Wife, huh?" laughed Follin. He had seen Eve as his wife many times in his dreams. "Do you really want to be my wife?" he asked.

"Yes," replied Eve, "ever since we first met."

Follin stretched and said, "Well, then, we'd better go see the Mayor and ask him to put our marriage into the Saoirse records. Then we'll visit the head families of the town. I'm sure to find some sort of work with them. They should be happy with the healing you've done with their families. You'll be a good luck charm for me. When I left home all those years ago I was a fool, but now I think I've grown up a bit." He smiled. "And I'm married now, too."

———

Follin had been absent from the village on his vision quest for seven years. Despite the devastation of the wars, and the plague that followed, there were still enough people in the township who remembered the awkward, gangly fool who could not read, write nor catch a ball. Today Follin walked tall, his head held high as he walked with his wife through the middle of town. At the third house his inquiries for work met with success.

"Well, well, well, it's young Follin. I see you've returned to your family home and married that lovely young healer girl. She has become a valued member of our township. Not only have you grown and filled out but you seem to have matured somewhat. I have heard that you now know a little of your numbers and letters, and that you have a way with people, too." The aged Knight, Sir Cecil, smiled lightly. "I may have some work for you. My House Steward has taken ill and I need someone to manage my household. Be here tomorrow at dawn and you can start with managing the day staff for me. They can be a bit of a handful and they'll play tricks, but if you're the man for the job, you'll have them to their tasks soon enough. If not, then I'll know about it by lunchtime." Sir Cecil looked at the young man steadily.

Follin held his gaze and said clearly, "Thank you, sir." He walked briskly out of the building and rejoined Eve waiting at the tavern.

"And so? Did Sir Cecil give you a job?" Eve's head was tilted to one side and a questioning smile played across her face. When Follin failed to answer straight away her smile was quickly replaced by a worried frown.

It was Follin's turn to smile. "Of course he did. Have you no faith, my dearest? I'm to try out as House Steward and run Sir Cecil's household staff." He grinned at her. Together they chatted over their hot coffee, a new beverage, brought in by seagoing traders. It was strangely invigorating but horrid in taste. Putting his cup down Follin politely said, "Dearest, next time, can we just have tea?"

The days were long as Follin worked hard to solve the many and varied problems of Sir Cecil's household. At first the staff were not happy with their new washerwoman; next, it was the squabbles amongst the younger staff and the older staff, followed by a stream of complaints of one form or another. Each was met by Follin with a logical application of firm but empathic instruction. By the end of his second week, Sir Cecil called Follin in for what he thought would be a review of his performance.

"Son," he said, "you've performed extremely well. I deliberately threw you into the deep end and you've come up trumps. Sadly, I have just received an urgent request for your services. I believe you will receive an important visitor very soon. It is with much regret that I have to let you go." Sir Cecil would not be pushed to give further explanation, only saying that a higher power, an old friend of his, had requested Follin's services.

The young man stood to shake the aged Knight's proffered hand, and sombrely made his way home. It was dark, it was cold, and he felt bewildered at this sudden turn of events. By the time he arrived home, Follin was frightened - no, he was terrified. What if this was just an excuse to get rid of him? What if Sir Cecil was really displeased with his performance but was too polite to tell him directly? What if this was all a terrible joke?

Follin walked into the cottage, changed into his work rags without speaking, then walked outside to weed the garden. He could not say a thing to Eve. He was afraid that what he feared most was true and then he would lose Eve, too. The sensitive young man needed time to think and he could do that best in the garden - alone.

A few minutes after Follin had left the house to contemplate his future, Eve heard a knock on the door. A dark-haired, well-presented young woman, a court Page, asked to speak with 'The Fool'.

"I'm sorry, but the only other person here is my husband, his name is Follin. How may I help you?" asked Eve, a little taken aback by the fine clothes and the formal manners of the pretty young lady at her front door.

"I have a message for... Follin, from an old friend of his, The Emperor," stated the Page.

Eve stood quietly as she considered the strange request. A few moments later she remembered her manners and invited her visitor inside. She took her to stand by the warm fire.

"I'll get my husband, he's outside tidying up the garden beds. Wait here, please, while I fetch him."

The young page studied the humble cottage and was pleased to see that it was well kept and clean. This was information that she would take back to her master. She was startled out of her reverie when she heard her name.

"Alice! Why, look at you, how you've grown. You were just a wee child the last time I saw you." Follin stepped forward to embrace the young lady warmly.

"Eve, this is Alice. She was one of the little girls running around the Empress' and Emperor's castle when I was there years ago." Follin spoke excitedly, this was such a surprise. "So what news do you bring? Is all well with my friends, the Empress and Emperor?"

Alice laughed as she was placed gently back on her feet. "Fool... I mean, Follin, it is lovely to see you again. All the girls still talk of that handsome young man who stole our hearts." She was flirting with him but quickly remembered where she was and became formal. "The Emperor has instructed me to inform you that he wishes to see you as soon as possible. He also instructed me not to leave without you and your wife. We can leave as soon as you're both ready."

Eve looked at Page Alice, then at her husband. "We can't do that. I mean, we just got married, and now Follin has a very good job with Sir Cecil. If he doesn't turn up for work tomorrow he'll lose his one and only job. And besides," she paused to add with emphasis, "if he doesn't go to work tomorrow he'll never be trusted in the village again. We might as well kiss our home here goodbye."

Follin realised he should have told Eve what Sir Cecil said to him, but he had been afraid and confused. He had not been sure that his new wife would stay with him if she knew he had lost his job, even if it was for service with a 'higher authority'.

Alice eyed Eve for a few seconds. "Eve, I was instructed to offer Follin employment with the Emperor himself. He said that he had positions for you both. He asked me to tell you that you might not return to this village for some time if you accept his offer."

Both Follin and Eve stood, clearly perplexed, this didn't seem possible. A job offer from the Emperor?

Follin put his arm around his wife and pulled her in to his side protectively. "Alice, is this true? The Emperor wants to give us employment? We'll both be working for him in his castle? Did he say what we'll be doing?"

"Hey, slow down, and yes, he did say all that." The dark-haired Page gave a warm smile. "You'll be studying in each of the Tarot Kingdoms, and Eve will be apprenticed to the alchemist, Mage Hermes, the Emperor's healer. Sir Cecil's letter commending your performance with his household has already arrived at the Emperor's castle. The Emperor was very pleased with his report. Follin, please, don't let this opportunity slip through your hands," she said, watching his reaction. She also watched Eve out of the corner of her eye.

Follin breathed deeply and exhaled slowly. He repeated the act twice more as he settled the nervous butterflies fluttering in his stomach.

"Eve, my love, I was afraid to speak to you when I arrived home this evening," he began with a nervous rush of words. "Sir Cecil told me that he had to let me go from his employment because I was needed elsewhere. I was so worried that I didn't know what to do. That's why I went out to the gardens, to think and clear my mind."

Eve blinked then set her face ready for what might happen next. All this was so new to her that her own insecurities threatened to pierce her veil of calmness.

Follin turned to Alice. "Alice, would you care to share our evening meal?" He waited for her reply. When she nodded, he continued. "I need to meditate on this matter. The Empress herself often reminded me not to make a decision in haste. I'll retire for just a short while to ponder before giving you my decision."

He turned to his wife once more. "I'm sorry if I upset you, dearest, I needed time alone. I would like to hear what you think before retiring to my meditation."

Eve was initially in mild shock, but now began to recover her senses on hearing her husband's explanation. "Husband of mine, whatever you decide to do I know it will prove to be the best thing for us. Personally, I can't wait."

Trying to suppress the growing excitement in her voice, Eve invited Alice to join her in preparing their evening meal, then to help her pack their meagre belongings. Follin smiled with relief as he walked outside to sit quietly in the woodshed to compose his mind.

'I've not connected with my inner world for guidance like this for a while,' he said to himself. *'I'll contact the High Priestess and ask her for advice.'*

As his breathing slowed he felt himself entering his personal sanctuary, a clearing in the forest. It was his old hermit cottage, a humble stone-walled hut with green grass sods covering its roof. He stopped to admire his handiwork: above the door was a carved oak beam showing a woman sitting beside a lion on a river bank.

He breathed slowly as he dropped deeper into trance. This time he found himself in the High Priestess's Sanctuary. He called softly for Hera, the High Priestess.

"It is The Fool who is not so foolish now. Welcome, Follin," he heard her soft, melodic voice inside his head, just as he had many times before. "What do you wish from me?"

"High Priestess Hera, I've married a beautiful and honourable woman, I seek your blessing on our union," was his first request.

"You had it before you asked. What else do you request?"

"I have been invited to serve the Emperor, in his castle. Eve has been invited to study the art of healing with the Emperor's alchemist, Mage Hermes. I seek your wisdom on this."

"Ah, the Emperor. If it is his wish then it would be wise to join him in his household." The soft voice paused as she waited for Follin to process her words. "Now I have something to ask of you in return." Follin felt her mind caress his. "My forest glade is small, my Sanctuary is vulnerable. Ignorance and greed have permeated the minds of mankind. The warlords of the kingdoms surrounding our Empire are destabilising its harmony. I wish for you to help me heal and protect it. Will you do this for me?"

Follin's mind wandered back to his time in that same glade and of the wonders he experienced there in trance under her guidance. "Of course, your will is mine to fulfil. It will be done if it is within my power."

"I have one other request, my son. Eve has powers that need to be awakened. She may never discover these powers without Mage Hermes' help, and mine."

Slowly the High Priestess's image and fragrant, forest perfume faded, and Follin felt the chill of the night air. He could hear Eve's voice calling for him to join them for dinner.

When they had cleaned up after their meal, Alice pulled a piece of paper from her bodice. The paper was folded into many squares.

"What is this?" asked Follin as she handed it to him.

"The Emperor asked me to hand this to you when you agreed to join him. It's a map of your journey. This first picture here, see it? It signifies the beginning. He said that it was destined. See that Pentacle, the circle with the star inside? It means that your first adventure is in my kingdom, the Pentacles Kingdom."

Both Follin and Eve stared at the paper. It contained images. The first was a hand reaching out of a cloud, clasping a Pentacle. Below was a garden with white flowers. They looked like lilies, perfect in every way, as though crafted by a master artisan. Beyond the garden was a mountain range.

"Ready?" asked Alice.

"Now?" Follin and Eve asked in unison.

"Yes," replied Alice.

Follin looked to Eve, who nodded.

"Look closely, my dear friends. Look closely and walk with me through the garden gate. Come with me on this journey to the Emperor's castle in the foothills of those mountains, the mighty Hindamars." Page Alice held their minds as she had been taught. The three left the humble cottage to find themselves standing before the tall, imposing walls of the Emperor's castle.

"Alice?" asked Follin, his eyes wide with some trepidation, "are we still in our Mystic Isle? I have a feeling that this is the mainland, the land of the Tarot Empire."

———

** *This introduces Follin at the start of his journey through the Tarot Kingdoms with each representing one of the Tarot suits. Each Kingdom presents unique and specific lessons for Follin and his wife, Eve.*

2nd revised and edited edition August 2020

Also available as an audiobook masterfully narrated by Jonathan Johns.

Chapter 15 - We live in two worlds

We live in two worlds but so few understand this and even fewer speak up about it. The 6 o'clock news certainly doesn't, and your parents and friends probably never told you either.

The first world is what you see around you now with your eyes open, it is the physical world. You know the rules quite well and how to survive in this world. For instance if you try to walk through walls you'll just get a sore nose.

The other world exists within your psyche, you access this other world when you close your eyes – the inner world. The rules there are different, very different.

In this world you are only limited by your imagination. You can travel through time to the future and back to the past. You can travel across great distances through space just by imagining you are there. This is possible using remote viewing techniques.

It truly is a world of magic, but everyone has to earn the right to enjoy the magic it delivers. You earn it by working hard at your relaxation and meditations, by using specific techniques.

Leonie came to me crippled with anxiety, she struggled to even go near water, even for a shower. She had anxiety attacks just thinking about being near the edge of anything, heights terrified her. My goodness she sure had some problems and I wasn't sure I would be able to help. I needed to do some magic otherwise we'd get nowhere fast.

Sure, I could do some psychotherapy, maybe some hypnotherapy. But I really like to get results and that meant I would need to take her where few have gone before - Pluto's Cave, the portal to her inner world.

Leonie was a meditator and an artist which gave me an idea, so I described working with her Inner Child. She was interested so we started working with her inner selves straight away.

That helped a lot, as I knew it would. But I was now intrigued, Leonie worked so easily in her inner world that I decided to introduce her to astrology and the archetypes. I knew it would help take her towards full healing.

I usually start by introducing the two most powerful archetypes I know of, the Sun and the Moon. If you haven't already studied my free introduction to 'Psychological Astrology' course then now is the time because you'll find out why I use these two archetypes first.

I'll stick with her experiences with the Sun in this book. For Leonie the Sun was a majestic male, powerful yet gentle. On my suggestion he took her to his home, a mansion on the edge of an enormous mountain, much like a Tibetan Monastery high up in the Himalayas. Leonie was afraid of water and so on her very first visit he took her to his swimming pool and asked her to walk in.

Terror, sheer terror arose inside her and she told him she wouldn't, couldn't do it. But he coaxed her, walked with her holding her hand as she went into the water, deeper and deeper as she went completely under water. Finally Leonie was able to sit on the floor of the pool. There he left her and as her terror rose he spoke soothingly to her. Eventually she relaxed and watched as bubbles, shapes and patterns formed, mesmerised she lost her fear. Over a number of meditations she completely lost her fear of water, swimming pools, showers, baths and the ocean.

Leonie was afraid of heights too so what did he do on her first session to heal this phobia? You guessed it, he took her to sit on the edge of the cliff beside his mansion. She sat with her feet dangling over the edge of the mountain. It was so high up that the clouds were way down below her. Once again the Sun sat with her until she was ready to sit there alone, and that is exactly what she did.

This was just the beginning of her adventures in her inner world. It is so real that it's influence on the outer world is significant. If nothing changes in your outer world then you are just imagining - but then, the inner world begins with imagination so keep doing.

Chapter 16 - Tarot Scrying Meditation - The Hierophant

This post comes from one of my tarot meditations which one day I will eventually turn into a book. Until then please enjoy my wyrd musings.

Tarot cards entered Europe around the 1400's (http://www.druidry.org/library/history-playing-cards-and-tarot) which was only possible after paper (cardboard) was mass produced and freely available. These cards arrived in Europe most probably via the Silk Road from China (and possibly trade with India). Most trade at that time was channelled through the ports of Venice where the powerful trading families of Italy and Venice controlled most of the trade routes.

At that time people played games, one of the main distractions people had from their boring and mundane existence. They would drink, gamble or play games of some sort. Just imagine today how life would be quite boring without TV or mobile phones.

Games such as shuffleboard, dice, games played on a board particularly chess, draughts, and backgammon. Common games of strength and skill included bowling, wrestling and archery.

But games of chance, like gambling, held most people's interest. At one time the Pope banned dice because of its role in gambling, violence, murder, drinking and swearing. When *playing cards* arrived, the people of Italy in particular, couldn't get their hands on enough packs of cards to indulge in another distraction, and a fantastic distraction it was for the rich as well as the poor.

At this time all cards were hand-made, there were no printing presses. Therefore getting your hands on a pack of cards was expensive and therefore very difficult. Eventually, from the many non-standard packs of cards which could number anything from 50 to a 100 cards, there came more standard forms. Initially each artist could draw whatever they liked, but there soon developed a series of standardised pictures and suits: four suits, court cards and numbered cards. But, and this is the interesting part, they also had 'trick' or 'trump' cards. In Italian they were called 'trionfi' or 'tarocchi' cards – these are the Major Arcana cards of the tarot deck.

At that time Monks and student Catholic priests, seminarians, began to develop their own card decks. Back then there were no fixed number of cards but they did have four suits and many trump cards (tarocchi).

These monks, seminarians and priests were big on gambling, it helped pass the time, soon created their own card games. Cards were played just as voraciously as dice games by every layer of the Catholic Church along with many other forms of gambling (and other means of distraction). Priests and monks were no different to anyone else then, as they are no different today, in their desire for distraction and entertainment.

We are talking the 1400's here, all card decks were hand made, hand drawn and the variety of card images was enormous. Only some of the decks had cards numbered from 1 to 10 and some included Jack to King, but most had extra cards called trump cards, 'tarocchi' or tarot cards. The trumps were sometimes used as a fifth suit: Hearts (Cups), Diamonds (Pentacles), Clubs (Wands), Spades (Swords) and Trumps (Major Arcana).

These extra triumph cards could 'trump' or defeat another card and were sometimes used as wild cards to win a hand. They each had different roles and different strengths. Today we see these same decks with UNO and Pokemon - they have tarocchi or trumps too. The Joker in our decks today is a tarocchi card used to 'trump' other cards.

If you examine our current tarot decks you'll find the Italian merchant family's influence. You will also see the strong Catholic Church influence. The Emperor, Empress, Hierophant, High Priestess, Chariot, Judgement, Temperance, Hermit, Justice, Devil, Star and the list goes on. These hand drawn cards were soon commissioned by the rich Italian merchant families and created by professional artists. Only the rich could afford their own expensive tarot or playing cards.

The Rider-Waite-Coleman deck was basically a copy of the [Sola-Busca family deck from Milan](https://solabuscatarot1998mayer.wordpress.com/sola-busca-waite-smith-tarot/), Italy, created around the 1490's.

So it seems the tarot did not come from Egypt at all, nor was it invented by the Gypsies, nor were they secret or magical of origin. But that does not detract you from using them to open the door to your inner world of magic.

You can still find tarocchi games today, particularly the older traditional games, played in households throughout Europe. They are just cards, but absolutely amazing when used as tools for personal growth and insight.

The Hierophant

Whereas the High Priestess is the feminine of the Pope, the Hierophant IS the Pope. He represents the outer path to spirit which is the application of those qualities that allow you to journey the inner path. We do this through study, education and engaging in the traditional inner and outer spiritual journey.

The Hierophant represents one side of the culture of study and we acknowledge that if you want to learn something you first need to learn how to acquire knowledge. This is the outer path of learning.

We could say that the Hierophant's path is the path of passing knowledge down from one generation to the other. In this case it started with the shaman many millennia ago and continued through the varied religious orders we know of throughout history.

Study of any kind requires rigour, dedicated practice, self discipline, determination and long hours of rote learning. The Hierophant is the eternal student of life yet he also represents the eternal teacher.

The Pope of the Roman Catholic Church represents God's voice on Earth. Yet he is more than just a voice, he is an entire culture from centuries of dedicated learning. Drawing this card suggests that we need a method of study to thoroughly understand our chosen field of knowledge.

From Arthur Edward Waite, *'The Pictorial Key To The Tarot'* (1911) illustrated by Pamela Colman Smith:

"*He wears the triple crown and is seated between two pillars, but they are not those of the Temple which is guarded by the High Priestess. In his left hand he holds a sceptre terminating in the triple cross, and with his right hand he gives the well-known ecclesiastical sign which is called that of esotericism, distinguishing between the manifest and concealed part of doctrine. It is noticeable in this connexion that the High Priestess makes no sign. At his feet are the crossed keys, and two priestly ministers also kneel before him. He has been usually called the Pope, which is a particular application of the more general office that he symbolizes. He is the ruling power of external religion, as the High Priestess is the prevailing genius of the esoteric, withdrawn power.*"

If we continue along this line connecting Christianity with the evolution of the tarot symbology we clearly see that there is a role for this card, the Hierophant. He becomes the wise, stern, disciplined counsel of the Catholic Church itself. But we have the freedom to choose to interpret him as a wise teacher or mentor. In this guise he is the Druid, shaman, yogi guru, zen shike, taoist sage, wicca witch and wizard.

The positive expression or manifestation of this card is quite important, to become wise you had best choose a method that teaches you how to be wise. It helps if you have a teacher, a mentor or wise advisor to assist you in your endeavour. The Hierophant is the mystic's mentor showing how one needs to study to become the Adept, the Master.

Is the Hierophant a master? Not necessarily but he can teach you the process you need to follow to become a master yourself. That is his strength, listen to his wise guidance and counsel.

My meditation:- "I am back at school, 9 years old, a sensitive little boy. My teacher is a brute who enjoyed tormenting his students. Like all bullies he took great pleasure in the psychological and physical torture of those who couldn't defend themselves, and he found his victims in small children. This time I know that it is going to be quite different, I am no longer a small, defenceless child.

I wait in his store room and quickly find his cane: a long thick stick I remember so well. I stand by the door so that he won't see me. When the door opens I slam it shut, he is trapped. Up comes my cane and down it flicks, again and again, he cries like so many small boys cried under his hand for decades. I don't stop, it goes on and on until it fades and I feel light and free and fall asleep.

I now find myself in the bush (forest) and I am sitting in front of a campfire with a pot of water hanging by a stick above. The Hierophant is beside me, watching me.

"Had a dream son?" he asks. I look at him, I can tell he knows of my childhood experiences and this dream of revenge.

"Sometimes a teacher is not honourable but a coward, someone who preys on those who can't defend themselves. He affected you in many ways. I too am glad he's gone. But his legacy lives on inside all those who suffered under his lust for power and pleasure," says the Hierophant.

The Hierophant took a sip of his hot tea before continuing. *"There are many wounded souls who felt the touch of the bully in institutions across the planet. It's sad that my profession have helped perpetuate such misery over thousands of years. But it is in man's nature to wrestle power from others for self gain and pleasure."*

We listen to the sounds of nature around us. *"Don't worry, you have done your best to ease the suffering of others, now it is time to sit and enjoy the sunset."*

This meditation was followed up by another tarot archetype but I shall include that in a later book. It is important to note that your meditations with the tarot cards will be unique to your own specific life experiences, I wouldn't expect yours to be like mine.

Chapter 17 - The Asteroid Goddesses - Ceres / Demeter

A lovely member of our community suggested this topic, the Asteroid Goddesses, so I am starting with my personal favourite.

I am a rather conservative astrologer and try to avoid adding too many points to the chart. Too much clutter in the chart causes it to become too noisy, too distracting. If you stick to your own chart and perhaps that of your family and friends, doing astrology as a hobby, then this doesn't necessarily apply. You have plenty of time to examine each point and cross reference personal experiences, read up and research the background mythology and then check it against your family and friends charts.

However, as a professional astrologer time becomes a luxury. There is also the concern that by using extra points in a chart the astrologer isn't personally connected and that may lead to making mistakes. That is an important consideration for all professionals: know your limitations.

When I began my practice as a psychologist one of my mentors made that point very clear: *'if you don't know something refer on to someone who does, know your limitations'*.

By now you probably know that I meditate and take others into their inner world as well, that's where Pluto's Cave comes from. My world is the 8th house and being a Leo means that what I do I like to do properly and hate making mistakes.

Ceres is the Roman name for the Greek Goddess, Demeter, she is the mother of Persephone, the young lady kidnapped by Pluto and taken into his realm, the Underworld. Ceres was so grief stricken that she scoured the world looking for her missing daughter. When she learned that Pluto held her prisoner in Hades, the Greek word for the Underworld, she went straight to the top, to Jupiter. There she told him to do something, or else!

(Pluto is the Roman name for the Greek God, Hades, and Hades is generally called 'Hell'. Jupiter is the Roman name for the Greek God, Zeus).

Jupiter said he couldn't do anything because his brother, Pluto, wasn't going to give her up. Ceres told him that that wasn't good enough and she was now going to stop doing her job until she had her daughter back. No more fertility, sunshine, harvest, happiness and all other things that she ruled.

The winter came early and the crops died, people and animals stopped conceiving and everyone on earth became very annoyed at the Gods. Jupiter became very worried so he called for his brother, Pluto. It was decided that Persephone would stay above ground with her mother for six months of the year and below with Pluto for the other six months.

Persephone is another Goddess of power, she co-rules Hades with her husband, Pluto. They both have special qualities but we won't go there today.

Many tarotists see Ceres as the Empress card in the Tarot Major Arcana, she represents feminine power, the power to create, to give life, bring into fruition, to birth. She also represents emotional support and family, dedication, love and loyalty. In fact, if you study the Greek Goddesses you will see this common thread, they all love and they all create. Ceres seems to be the one who manifests this in our outer world with greater clarity - what she does is make things real.

I have Ceres in my 12th house, for me that is a cave on the beach and inside sits the one-eyed Cyclops. I first met him when I was writing my book, *Psychological Astrology And The Twelve Houses*. He and I sometimes sit together in my meditations and I curl up in his arms. He is like the BFG, the Big Friendly Giant. He says he protects me from the wild world outside his cave. He often reminds me, '*it's dangerous out there*'.

One day I decided to visit Ceres in my 12th house. I saw her sitting at a large loom weaving a shawl. It was like a big fish net women wear around their shoulders. The wool was soft like cashmere, superfine wool, and it was thick and so much like a fish net that I had to ask her what it was for.

She handed it to me and told me to wear it. It curled around me like a cocoon and I fell into a deeper trance. I use it sometimes and that is what it does, it takes me deeper into trance in my meditations.

I also met her in a dream. I had worked the previous few nights setting up a meeting with her in my dreams and finally it happened. It was a little weird because I was dreaming an ordinary dream, as we usually do when we sleep.

It was in a shopping mall with crowds of people milling about and this woman just stood out. I was walking past a bright-eyed, auburn haired woman and I just stopped in my tracks, mesmerised by her look. She was very real, where everyone else was busy she was serene and present, she caught my eye and I was drawn to her.

As I was standing there looking at her, I thought to myself that I knew her from somewhere. That somewhere might be my inner world?

Ceres looked into my eyes to make sure I was paying attention and told me that I would achieve everything I wanted in this life, 'and more'. Yes, even astrologers need a second opinion.

She is very special to me, I have met her a few more times and each time I come away feeling validated and accepted, knowing my journey continues. Perhaps you too could visit your Ceres and ask a few questions - what does she say to you?

Chapter 18 – My black blob experience

Crossing into dimensions beyond the physical can happen when we sleep. Astral Travel and Out Of Body (OOB) experiences have been described by many people, Robert Monroe is one famous person who was able to fall asleep and leave his body to enter these other dimensions. He wrote books on his adventures and ran the Monroe Institute teaching people how to do it. This is the fellow who produced the Hemi-synch audio system for enhanced meditation.

I began learning tai chi in 1980, after about 6 months of practice things happened that changed the course of my life forever. I found I would wake up in my dreams. At first it felt strange and so I asked my tai chi master who just said, *"keep doing tai chi and you will understand more"*. I did and in time I began to learn some of the 'rules' of astral travel: don't fixate on anything, just keep it smooth, breathe chi out through your feet, hands or head if you get stuck, etc.

Time after time I would wake up with tingling legs, so itchy that I had to scratch them which of course made no difference. It was from the enormous amount of chi, kudalini, that surged through my body when I astral travelled.

One of the other tai chi students told me that he needed to learn tai chi to protect himself because he feared falling sleep. He would stay awake for as long as he could, 2, 3 nights in a row until exhaustion got to him and he had to sleep. He would then find himself in a blackness that had an 'evil fear' embedded in it. The fear was so great he would wake in panic.

I struggled to understand this because nothing like that ever happened to me. That is until the time I woke in a blackness of space, so black I couldn't see a thing. I could feel an evil presence and then the fear began to rise inside of me. Luckily I had been doing tai chi long enough to have developed an ability to 'centre' and before this presence touched me, I disappeared. I don't know where I went but it was somewhere that this evil presence was unable to follow.

The sensation of centering feels like someone grabbing or punching my navel area. This is the part of the body that we meditate on to draw chi or energy into our body, into the 'chi furnace'. It is called the dan tien or 'center point'. In Chinese medicine and in taoist tantra it is known as the power or life force generator of the body. Centering is a basic meditation practice and I found out why it was so important that night.

Only one other time did I have a frightening experience. My baby daughter was asleep across the hallway in her bedroom and for some reason I sort of woke up but I wasn't really awake. I was out of my body but sitting up in bed. I sensed the presence of 2 black blobs, energy beings, crawling along the hallway outside my bedroom. They certainly weren't human just black blobs of some kind.

I couldn't hear anything but I could feel them searching, searching for energy. I realised that they were sniffing for food, their food was human life force.

I was sitting up but my body was lying in the bed asleep and I was curious. I had never sensed these blobs before and yet here they were right outside my bedroom. The door was closed and I instinctively knew that this wouldn't stop them. At that moment I realised these beings, these blobs of blackness, were after me! Suddenly, my navel centre went 'crunch', and I disappeared.

I have no idea where I went but some minutes later I came back to consciousness and once again I was sitting out of my body in the bed again. My young aura was bright and full of lovely, tasty life force. The black blobs immediately sensed that I was back in my body and lunged for me. They came straight through the wall. I freaked out and my navel centre went 'crunch' again and I disappeared once more.

Minutes or hours later, I have no idea which, I came back to my body. Again I was out of my body sitting up above my sleeping self. I scanned the hallway, my daughter's bedroom, the other bedrooms. I sent my senses around the house and yard, nothing there. The blobs of black energy had gone. They had given up and left for someone easier, in search of someone else's life force.

Now before I finish this chapter I will tell you who they went after. Some time after this experience I was out of body tending to a drug addict who had blacked out in the street. I got there before the ambulance but at the same time as those darn life-sucking black blobs. They stood back away from him, and me, about two meters away. They seemed to be patiently waiting. I now had more energy than they did and they no longer bothered me. Funnily I had no fear, it just didn't occur to me to be afraid of them.

I gently touched this young person's third eye and pushed energy into him. I then disappeared back to my body asleep in bed. I only hope that what I did was enough to save this guy from losing some of his life force. Sadly, I don't believe that I saved him from his fate of drug addiction.

What are these black blobs? I really don't know except that they feed off people's energy. They don't kill people or even harm them. I guess they live on a dimension that has no other energy supply. I was just a tasty morsel that they would have feasted on if they had caught me, but even then I doubt I would have noticed the loss of energy. I probably would have woken next morning just like I normally would. They aren't interested in killing people but just have a need for a little of their life force.

So please don't freak out and fear going to sleep. This story was to show you what can be done by someone who walks the mystics path. We are always going to be challenged in life but remember that there are far worse life-forms on earth called 'nasty people'. We call them narcissists, bullies, sociopaths and psychopaths. You will meet them at home, at work and in the community, many of them run our political system. They will certainly do far more damage to your self-worth and self-esteem than those little black suckers.

Chapter 19 - Astrology cycles

I practised as an astrologer for many years before I studied psychology. These days I can sometimes look at a chart and see the person's soul. I am not as good as I would like to be but it does get easier the more charts I read and the more I study and meditate. The past and future is there, what an incredible instrument astrology is.

One thing I had to come to terms with was that astrology is all about cycles. The chart itself is a circle, a metaphor for the movement of the planets and constellations around us, it cannot be anything else. Its beauty is its simplicity.

I read the chart by turning the planets into people. The chart house is where they live and act, and the sign is the personality they adopt. Thus a Cancer Moon conjunct (next to) Saturn in the 8th house demonstrates how the person acts emotionally (Moon in Cancer), where they will express their emotions, and as the 8th house is in the house of transformation and crisis, they will act emotionally to most life situations. Hopefully they will work to transform those events and emotions into life changing events. They will also remember every crisis they have ever had. Because of their extreme sensitivity life hurts, stabbed by cruel barbs of suffering.

Saturn sitting next to the Moon, that dark, sober, and depressing bring-you-down-to-earth planet, indicates that this person has great difficulty sharing emotions. They lock their tender feelings inside, no matter how much they hurt they won't show it.

If you had this configuration (and there is much more in everyone's astrology chart than Moon conjunct Saturn, of course) then I know it will take a lot of trust before you will open up and share. I know that you will have a depth of understanding of emotion and will have an intuitive understanding of pain and emotion. You will slowly become a deep thinker and have a deeper understanding of life than most. As you grow older you will be able teach others how to manage life because you have lived with pain and suffering and learned how to manage.

This is just your birth or natal configuration but of course the planets and constellations never stop, they are in perpetual motion in the heavens above. Eventually Saturn will have moved until it appears opposite its natal position, across from the 2nd house (the house opposite the 8th where Moon and Saturn reside). What happens now?

Your life cycle has moved to bring new lessons. Transiting (or moving) Saturn opposite the natal, or birth Moon, triggers all sorts of nurturing issues (Moon) under the doom and gloom personality of Saturn.

Saturn is the God of Time, Cronus, and his influence on you is to challenge you to address the long-standing issues you have with nurturing. This could be your own mothers controlling behaviour as a child, belittling and humiliating, or your marriage in which nurturing plays a big part. It is also your ability to nurture yourself and others.

I now know that these issues are challenged in many ways. Some on the surface, such as friendships, have even started to break down. Or it could be deeper in your unconscious in which you feel you have never been nurtured or loved since childhood, and are becoming depressed and needy.

What happens when the cycle ends? It starts another, a new one, on another dimension that was not addressed previously. Cycles exist to allow you time to work on issues that need to be fixed, then you can shift gears and change to the next issue that needs addressing.

When you are reborn I believe that you simply start a new cycle. You may choose to reincarnate to work on specific issues in the emotional cauldron of planet Earth, or go to another planet or dimension to learn or resolve others. I am not sure when they stop, maybe they do, maybe they don't.

Chapter 20 - Stopping the world

'Stopping the world' is a nice descriptive term that actually does what it says. You reinforce your perspective of your world by repeatedly talking to yourself, reminding yourself of what your world is, what it consists of. If you can stop talking to yourself you can stop reinforcing the limits of your world. This metaphor comes from Carlos Castaneda's stories of his sorcerer mentor, Don Juan.

If you don't reinforce your world beliefs you can change these beliefs. This takes time and practice and is not for everyone, it is frustrating and quite difficult.

How do you stop your internal dialogue? You do this by deliberately relaxing, going for walks, looking not thinking, free-form meditating until you fall into a blank 'space'. It is feeling rather that thinking. It is about changing your habitual patterns of thinking with specific dedicated practices.

One of the first things to happen for you is the acceptance of new beliefs, of new possibilities. The world may not really be what you have been led to believe by the 6 o'clock news.

Once you have seen various possibilities you can begin to change. If you have a limiting belief, for instance, that you can't possibly swim in the ocean for fear of sharks, you never will. But if that possibility changes then you have broken your 'world belief'. One day you will swim in the ocean and damn the sharks.

This is a simple example but it really isn't rocket science either. Seek to deliberately practice the slowing of your thoughts by going for a walk every day, look and feel rather than analyse. Doing these exercises helps you enter the 'alpha state' which I have discussed in this book and elsewhere. Training to produce strong alpha brainwaves is essential for both healthy living and to change your beliefs. Alpha is a transition brainwave pattern which elite performers use to enter the zone. It is also called the 'resting state of the brain'.

One way to stop the world is to observe yourself when someone is talking to you. Observe your own internal chatter. If you find yourself critiquing their conversation then you are not listening but reinforcing your own world belief.

I find it challenging to always be present, empathic and unconditional while someone explains their issues to me. To be able to mentally step back and listen, to cease my own internal dialogue and not critique is not easy, but it does get easier with practice.

If I start to critique while someone is talking then I am not very useful to them. I miss things and I am not open to my intuition, which is what I pride myself on. I can go places inside their world by being present while they explain their issues to me. Their key words and concepts open my mind to their hurts, and more importantly, to their healing. It is like Sherlock Holmes and his 'mind palace', putting pieces of their puzzle together, intuitively, as they talk.

Stopping the world is a foundation technique for going further across the consciousness divide. It allows you to focus without being disturbed by your own internal chatter which becomes noise that disturbs your intuitive process.

This is a valuable technique for meditators as well, close your eyes and feel your body relax. Just doing that can shift you out of your head and into your body – not thinking just feeling. Being in the body generally leads to a cessation of internal dialogue. Just feeling and being, this is when you can stop this world to go into other worlds.

Chapter 21 - Dr Carl Jung - an introduction

Through Carl Jung's tireless study and writing, astrologers and psychologists are able to draw the curtain aside to look beyond human consciousness into the mystery of the unconscious. This is a short treatise on that great man to whom astrologers owe so much.

Carl Gustav Jung (26th July 1875 – 6th June 1961, aged 85) was born in Kesswil, Switzerland. He came from a very religious family and was the only surviving son of his father, a pastor of the Swiss Reformed Church. His uncles were also pastors. His mother was reported to be detached, suffering from bouts of depression. It became apparent that she had a mental disorder after spending time in a psychiatric hospital during Jung's early childhood.

His mother spent a lot of time in her bedroom and reported that spirits visited her at night. Jung was an only child until the birth of his sister some years later, he spend a lot of his childhood playing alone. Hid older brother had died soon after birth. Throughout his childhood Jung wrestled with conflicting religious thoughts.

It can be said that his childhood had a big influence on the development of his personality and his future ideas and philosophies. Jung described his childhood as very 'unhappy'. He said that he had suicidal tendencies, a death wish. This was possibly related to the depression he experienced from long separations from his mother while she was in mental institutions. He experienced strange thoughts and dreams that he remembered well into adulthood.

Jung had a fascination with death, the afterlife and the paranormal from an early age. The psychologist, Winnicott, diagnosed Jung with a childhood schizophrenia, due to his strange ideas.

Jung said that at age twelve he felt as if he had two personalities, one was his normal personality as a regular schoolboy, the other was of a wise old man. We can see the impact of those early developmental years in Jung's particular spiritual ideas in which he saw the world through a process of enlightenment which he termed Individuation, a form of personal spiritual growth.

As a teenager Jung described himself as being violent and aggressive. He experienced difficulty with people, friends, family members, teachers and peers. He explored his spiritual interests throughout his youth. He was a voracious reader in varied genres: mythology, spiritualism and archaeology. He studied medicine as his choice of career rather than theology like his father.

Carl Jung obtained his medical degree at Switzertland's oldest university, the University of Basel, specialising in psychiatry. Jung mentioned that he saw in psychiatry a way to integrate his own disturbed personality. He began his career as a psychiatrist working in the Burgholzi Psychiatric Hospital under Dr Eugen Bleuler, a friend of Sigmund Freud.

He was 30 years of age when he became familiar with the work of Dr Sigmund Freud. He publish his own papers on his views of the unconscious which he sent to Freud seeking the older man's opinion. The two psychiatrists eventually met in Vienna in 1907 talking for a full thirteen hours without a break. For the following six years, until May 1913, the two men had a close professional, as well as personal, association.

Freud, who was twenty years older than Jung, took the role of mentoring Jung, his younger colleague. It was expected that Jung would become a successor to Freud. In fact Freud prepared Jung to eventually become the leader of his prestigious psychoanalytic movement. Jung was the first president of Freud's own International Psychoanalytic Association and an editor of its related publication. Jung resigned the position as president after his separation from Freud.

Jung sought an historical context for the psychology of individuals, rather than simply focusing on their sexuality and unresolved childhood issues. In 1913 Jung and Freud ended their personal and professional relationship. This was hard for Jung who struggled to cope with their split thus initiating his own journey of self-analysis. He faced enormous self-doubt through those first few years of his personal psychotherapy.

During the time of their collaboration, Jung supported Freud's ideas, while he also continued to develop his own thoughts on the unconscious. Jung opened his own psychotherapy practice in 1909, and developed upon his earlier interest in psychic phenomena, spirituality, mythology, folk tales, legends and fairy tales. It was during this time that he began to criticise different aspects of Freud's theoretical work as well as his dogmatic attitude towards psychoanalysis. He felt that Freud did not encourage new ideas or views but rather expected his psychoanalytic ideas to be followed religiously.

During the 1st World War, Dr Jung served as an army doctor and commanded a prison hospital for British soldiers. This marked a turning point in his life as he had only recently split from his friendship with Freud in pursuit of validation for his own spiritual beliefs. It also initiated an existential crisis.

"*In 1913, at the age of thirty-eight, Jung experienced a horrible 'confrontation with the unconscious'. He saw visions and heard voices. He worried at times that he was 'menaced by a psychosis' or was 'doing a schizophrenia'. He decided that it was valuable experience and, in private, he induced hallucinations or, in his words, 'active imaginations' (http://en.wikipedia.org/wiki/Active_imagination). He recorded everything he felt in small journals. Jung began to transcribe his notes into a large red leather-bound book, on which he worked intermittently for sixteen years.*"
http://en.wikipedia.org/wiki/Carl_Jung

The crisis after his break with Freud led him to explore his personal unconscious and to delve deeper into his psyche. He particularly studied his dreams with great intensity. It brought him to examine the different spiritual, mythological and religious beliefs and philosophies that he incorporated into his 'analytical psychology'. Jung was fascinated with the mystics journey and went in search of alternative explanations such as astrology, alchemy, tarot and the Kabbalah. Later he extensively adapted occult ideas, names and symbols into his work.

Jung was involved in occult circles, such as spiritualism, through his cousin who was a spiritualist. He also reported having paranormal experiences himself. Jung took these ideas more seriously than most academics as he had a personal and a professional interest. He attended seances and studied spirit mediums which he knew from his mother's side of the family.

These experiences strongly influenced the development of his ideas, influencing them in an indirect manner as well. The seances influenced his idea of Individuation, a process that fused the fragmented parts of Self into a whole personality. His belief was that psychic experiences were produced by a link with the unconscious mind.

Jung had a strong interest in the spiritual world and beliefs. He examined ancient and animalistic native religions, fairy tales and psychic manifestations such as telepathy and premonitions of the future. Jung believed that the commonalities between myths, religions, fairy tales and legends were all manifestations of a unique psychic connection between every one of us. This he called the Collective Unconscious.

Sadly few psychologists consider using spiritual elements in their theories or therapies. Jung, despite his unorthodox teachings, has provided astrologers, clairvoyants, psychics, mystics and even the shaman with psychological and spiritual foundations in a period that was quite devoid of spiritual freedom. He gave us the valuable psychological concepts of Archetypes, the Collective Unconscious, Complexes, Extroversion and Introversion, Active Imagination and Individuation.

His legacy lives on through the work of the countless dedicated therapists and practitioners who strive to survive in a world that preaches money and power but ignores human spirituality.

If you wish to know more then I suggest that you start by studying the Greek myths which form the foundations of psychology as well as astrology.

I am in the slow process of collating material to write a book on astrology, Jung and the mystics journey. Make sure you subscribe to my newsletter to stay informed of its publication and receive your discounted purchase only for subscribers.

Chapter 22 - Astrology and family therapy

Every now and then I have a situation which is not all that it seems in the first session. Shirley (names changed) was exhausted, from work and from raising her very active only child, Max. Max was not popular at school, he complained that he had no friends at all. Max's teacher said he was bright and charming, they appreciated his intelligence and active personality, but his class mates saw him as a nuisance.

Max was diagnosed with Attention Deficit Hyperactivity Disorder, ADHD for short. His day begins by climbing into bed with his parents at the crack of dawn and then creating fun and havoc until bed time that night. Shirley tried all sorts of pills and potions, some of them worked, especially removing sugar and artificial additives from his diet. But Max wants the sweet things his mates have and so resists this prohibition by swapping his healthy lunch for his friend's sweets. He was on prescribed medication for ADHD which showed positive results back then.

There was another thing about Max, he was quite a genius. I expect that the world will be transformed by his brilliance not too far into the future.

His mother, Shirley, is a tireless worker, always rescuing someone at work or putting things right for others, she is quite the rescuer. However she is terribly concerned about her son's problems at school. Max's father, John, is a hard worker too and very bright. He encourages Max's interest in problem solving and information gathering. John's smart genes appear to have been inherited by Max along with his mother's compassion and determination.

So why did Shirley come for an astrology reading? She had problems at work that were dragging her down, but she was also worried about Max. Was he crazy? Was she crazy? And would she continue to cope with both Max and her own work pressures for much longer?

After some discussion she agreed to begin meditation and clinical hypnotherapy and psychotherapy. That was when she began to develop the tools to get through the worst of her personal challenges. It also started her on the path to create suitable strategies to manage Max. However, about 6 months later she returned with work related depression again.

Our personal problems often appear to be all-consuming, but within the problem lies the answer, like a rose among the thorns. With the help of psychotherapy Shirley didn't get her promotion but she did get her family back.

We examined the astrology charts of her entire family, Shirley, John and young Max. The first thing I did was reassure both John and Shirley that Max wasn't crazy and they really were worried that this was a possibility. After that discussion Shirley and John could relax a little.

Max's astrology chart showed that he was fine. He was hyperactive, yes, he was hyper-focused, loved routine but struggled to broaden his view of the world - he was typically self-centered, like most children, but with a greater intensity than most.

These significators were seen in his birth chart as a loaded 1st house, five planets in Capricorn and an emphasis on Aquarius.

The loaded 1st house and its Capricorn planets highlighted his self-centered focus on structure and order, his need for organisation and gave him Aries-like hyperactivity. Aquarius emphasised his mind and intuition as well as his hyperactivity, impulsivity, inattention and concentration problems. Max needed constant mental stimulation, otherwise his mind would wonder off to find something more interesting.

We then looked at the charts of both parents. It was obvious to me as an astrologer that there I would locate Max's inherited traits. John had an emphasis on the mind, Aquarius, Shirley gave him her Fiery Aries/Leo charm along with the 1st house drive and energy. Max was definitely the product of his parents. Our first problem was solved, no mental illness and he was very much his parent's child.

We were able to focus on possible problems that could arise as a consequence of his ADHD. These problems were clearly seen in his chart. Such things as heightened emotions, poor social skills, friendship difficulties and future relationship problems.

The process of first dealing with Shirley's personal and career problems, by easing her depression and determining alternatives to a career up the corporate ladder, helped her then focus on her underlying issue - Max, her one and only child. There was also a sex problem with her husband. We discussed a few male sex secrets and Shirley reported that she was now in control of the sex department (much to John's enormous satisfaction).

I never saw Max, but through his astrology chart we were able to settle Shirley's most immediate concerns. It was then possible to work on her deeper personal and relationship issues that had arisen in her marriage.

I find astrology an incredibly useful tool in understanding couples and families. It points out the personal issues each partner brings into the relationship as well as areas of compatibility and of disharmony.

Combining astrology and meditation / psychotherapy enabled us to assist the development of a suitable home program to manage Max's behaviour and to accommodate his parents needs. It was also helpful in developing a program of personal development for Shirley and John, it saved their marriage.

Chapter 23 – A quickie reading at a boat party

Astrologers are often caught short by well meaning acquaintances eager to show off their astrologer friend. Not enough time to deliver a proper presentation we need a simple method for just such an occasion. This is the story of how I managed an ambush on a cruise boat one evening.

Just picture this, a party in full swing, you are already 'three sheets to the wind' after a heavy day at work and in walks a mate with his new girl friend on his arm. Wanting to impress her the conversation goes along the lines of:

"Oh, you're an astrologer?! Purrr, can you guess my sign? Oh, I am having such a terrible year, can you tell me what the stars say, and when will I win the lottery?"

Ugh! Don't we loath it! I had no time to prepare myself so I went straight to the focal conflict points in her chart. In this case it was Venus conjunct the Ascendant and focal planet of a Yod. This gave me some useful insight into her relationship problems. This naturally led me to suggest some practical strategies, both psychological and realistic, which was just what she needed.

Here is a simple, short yet focused reading approach I used for this complete stranger who asked me about her money worries.

"It is quite clear that you focus on money matters with Venus and Taurus strongly placed. As well as this, Saturn has been transiting (crossing) from your 12th house into your 1st house over the past three years. Yes, Money Worries, you've not had it easy.

"Looking at your natal chart we see that Venus sits on your Taurus Ascendant, the sign that was rising on the horizon at the moment of your birth. Both Venus and your Ascendant are in Taurus so money is going to be a regular concern for the rest of your life. It is not that you never have money but you feel you really need lots of it to make you feel safe and secure. Venus, the ruler of Taurus, is sometimes known as the planet of money, cash flow and therefore security. It is also the planet of beauty, so maybe marrying a rich old man is the way to go. We can now look at your Venus, the focal planet of a Yod from Saturn and Jupiter.

"A Yod is a challenging planetary pattern which can make you feel as though you are regularly confronted by problems. The pressure builds up to breaking point then is released and all is good... until it builds up again. Saturn is the planet of contraction, caution and consequences, he wants you to be careful with your money and assets. Jupiter is the planet of plenty and of wild, irresponsible money-making schemes, the gambler, he wants you to get out there and spend.

"Can you imagine Saturn allowing Jupiter to spend money on get-rich-quick-schemes? No way. Therefore your Yod demonstrates a focal issue for you in this lifetime: to be able to handle your assets, be they beauty or money, carefully, and yet still satisfy Jupiter's needs for the odd fling on the horses.

"Aside from the Yod you also have a mini-stellium, three planets, residing in your 2nd house of security in Gemini. As Venus rules the 2nd house you will be feeling pressure to save and make more money. However Gemini sits on this cusp saying, 'Spend, drink, have fun, party 'til you drop!'

"We immediately see a conflict between the archetypes. The planets Venus and Jupiter and Gemini the zodiac sign, all want to be noticed and to have fun, while Saturn and Taurus want to save money and be more secure. This conflict manifests in your psyche as a need to spend and yet a need to save. You can go mad worrying about your money problems with an unresolved conflict like this.

"In therapy I would guide you into a light trance to talk to these archetypes. Now this may seem strange, but it is a powerful way for you to connect with the very archetypes that forms your universe and therefore your reality. I would imagine that Venus is quite confused. She would like to remain young and attractive but this costs money. Gemini would also like to be attractive but also wants you to get into life and party just as Jupiter does. Unfortunately the pressure from Saturn and Taurus builds up and up when their needs are not recognised.

"Saturn says: 'No, don't do it, think of the insecurity. Think of not having enough money to buy soap or makeup'. Jupiter will of course jump in and say that this is all unfair and requires a higher judgement of some kind.

"It can sometimes get busy during these inner conflict resolution sessions. You can gain insight into yourself using this approach, plus you will be able to work out some sort of compromise between the archetypes. This is basically the aim of all therapies, insight followed by resolution.

"If you can't get into trance to do this it would be beneficial for you to first understand that there is conflict and that you need to find a compromise between spending and saving. Work out a budget and stick to it, make sure you address Jupiter, Gemini and Venus' needs for beauty and pleasure. At the same time you need to allow Saturn and Taurus to feel that their concerns with saving and material security are also addressed. In other words spend carefully and learn some self discipline.

"Looking at your transits we see that you have already had several opportunities to make some great career and monetary gains over the past 12 months as Jupiter crossed both your Ascendant and Venus. Things have settled down now and you may have to wait another 2 years before you will feel prepared to challenge life again. Saturn has, after 3 years sitting quietly in his cave, just moved from the 12th house and into your first house of new beginnings. This is a rebirth in astrological terms.

"Saturn takes about 2 and a half years to transit through a house which means that you are now learning how to cope with the world at a different level. It is just like a caterpillar who has just transformed into a butterfly, she no longer has 20 legs to walk on. It is all quite new and somewhat stressful as things are no longer the way they use to be.

"I could go on forever here but basically this is a time for you to go slowly and gently because you are destined at this time to make some deep, sensible choices in life. Choices that will support you through the next 28 years. Yes, your money worries are real, but the answers and resources are inside you."

The above comes from a real conversation I had that night on the boat. It was spot-on, of course. Did she makes those changes? Did she do her meditations and negotiate with her archetypes? I don't know but I like to think that maybe she did. With study, practice and experience one day you too will be doing astrology readings on the fly. How? By remembering to locate and read the conflict points in the chart.

Chapter 24 - Emotional self defence—rock, water + boundaries

In Taoist exercises such as tai chi you learn to flow with the forces around and within you. You learn to centre, earth and expand your chi (life force) by moving in circular motions while breathing chi in specific ways. This enables you to act from within to achieve stability and harmony without.

To be like a 'rock' in life you learn to stand up for yourself, to say, "No" when you want to avoid doing what you really don't want to do. To be Water in life you learn to be adaptable and flexible in life, to say, "OK" when presented with something that you wish to participate in. Taoists seek to avoid conflict by flowing with the situation at hand, particularly when they are ambushed and unprepared.

For example, a rock state is applied when you don't want to join in an activity, or when being bullied, "No, that is enough." It supports you in conflict situations by ensuring that you don't crumble under a domineering force.

If you are being bullied or harassed by a fellow worker or manager you use your 'earthing' breath to create a rock state. Taoists train to withstand the anger and frustrations of an adversary and from within themselves. This helps you remain stable and centred, to be calm and peaceful within.

You can use your earthing breath to stabilise your chi in the lower half of your body, away from your heart and head. Then centre your breath in your centre point or dan tien to breathe chi into your arms and hands for physical self defence. Any excess of chi is sent out through your feet so that you will remain stable.

The rock state watches for signs of an impending assault and prepares you to defend yourself if necessary. It helps you flow and dance with your opponent. This may be simply a problem habit that you struggle to control, or an angry worker or neighbour. Rock is not conflict, it is to 'stand strong'.

You can use a water state when you need to be flexible and adaptable in difficult relationships with others. The Taoist avoids conflict by the practice of wu wei (non resistance) which means that you seek to flow like water with the situation.

The Taoist earths and centers their life-force using their breath which helps them gain clarity in their thinking. They let their energy guide them to find a solution to the problem organically, without stress. In other words, the decision is already made for them.

The water state is one of letting go and easing into the stream. It is harmony and helpfulness, particularly when someone asks for your support. Saying "Yes" to others in need, being mindful of your boundaries, is using the water state.

It is easiest to use your creativity and imagination in a water state. You can still earth and centre your breathing but you don't need to strengthen your aura for an impending assault as you would with the rock state. You can remain open and friendly, co-operative and helpful, but only enough to ensure that you aren't used or abused. You only give as much as you are prepared to give, no more and no less.

Boundaries—how much to give and take in life

My Taoist teacher would often say that we give and accept 100 grams (40 ounces) of pressure. This is a metaphor for the fulcrum, the mid point of a relationship. If you stand on one end of a balance beam or see-saw, and there is no equal weight on the other end, you would be out of balance. The giving of 100 grams in life means that you give that which is comfortable, no more and no less. If you give more than what makes you comfortable then you begin to feel off-balance, out of your centre. It is like leaning too far forward, you can fall over if you give even just a tiny bit more.

We were taught that in giving we receive, yes that's true, but in some relationships you give and find that others just take. It could be your child, manager, co-worker or partner who wants you to keep on giving without end. By continuing to give beyond the point in which you are happy you become uncomfortable, resentful. You learn to resist the impulse of guilt and to seek the balance point by becoming rock and say, *"No, it is time for you to do something for yourself, I won't do it all for you."*

Conversely when you don't give 100 grams you become lazy or self indulgent, selfish and greedy. Your partner asks for assistance or support and you give less than your comfortable 100 grams. This is how you may lessen yourself, you become someone who won't grow nor enjoy the benefits that comes with giving. By becoming a user and taker, greedy and selfish you create a personality that goes backwards, never expanding. To avoid the extremes of both situations, that of going backwards and that of being used and resentful, you seek the middle ground, the mid point, the 100 grams of giving and taking.

This is an important component of Taoism, to find the middle path in all things. You also learn to honour and respect yourself, your giving is with honour. You also instil honour and respect in others by your steadfast resolve to find the middle path in all dealings with them, you seek not to cheat nor to give foolishly.

The Taoist yin yang symbol is a perfect representation of balance and harmony. It can be said that one half is yang rock, the other yin water, each contains a little of the other. That small piece of the opposite reminds you to always consider where your balance point is.

By finding your middle path, and by dealing with people and situations with 100 grams, you set and establish **boundaries**. Boundaries are an essential emotional defence against being used and abused.

You use boundaries all the time, for example you don't talk about your sexual experiences to strangers, they're not within your personal or intimate circle of trust. You don't let your grocery lady into your home nor the bank clerk. There are certain rules and limits in your social and personal life that you vigorously enforce to ensure healthy emotional development and to avoid being violated.

The first boundary is your Social Space boundary. It is between 1 and 3 meters distant from you. When out in public you don't stand too close to others if there is room enough to stand equally between them and another person. You always move to the mid point. For instance when sitting in the cinema you usually sit half way between occupied chairs. It is considered rude and an invasion of boundaries and personal space to sit too close to someone when there are vacant seats further away. As more and more people are crowded into the space you allow them to get nearer without feeling invaded. This space is in proportion to the available space around you. It is OK to crowd a person when in a checkout line at the shopping mall, but not when walking in a park. Social space is usually less than a meter when at a party, any closer then becomes Personal Space.

Personal Space is less than one meter, within arms reach. You either invite someone into your personal space or you push them out. It is a very special space, anyone within that space can hit and hurt you. To allow someone in this close you trust that they will honour you enough not to hurt or harm you.

Tai chi chuan and chi kung breathing creates a powerful aura that contains this space. Once you have developed enough chi power you can control anyone within your personal space quite easily. The circular movement of tai chi is ideal for self defence for close-in fighting, as is Wing Chun and Bagua Kung Fu.

Intimate Space is when you are in an intimate relationship with someone. This is not for the mechanic or the cleaning lady, it is for your children, your lover, your mother and father, for anyone that you have a trusted and safe relationship with. The closeness is such that you intermingle your auras together bonding at many emotional and psychic levels.

Boundaries are important in counselling as it invokes transference and counter-transference which sees the projection of needs onto the other. By going further than your 100 grams you are, in one sense, overstepping your rights with that person. You might want more from them than they are prepared to give. In this case you give and give hoping for something in return. It may also be that they are asking for more than you are prepared to give. They ask and ask, becoming more and more demanding. If you give in you are setting yourself up for further abuse.

If in the helping profession you are working with people with emotional problems who generally have poor boundaries, they could very easily turn on you and hurt you. They could set you up and knock you down if you don't have strong professional boundaries.

Always be aware of your boundaries, don't give more than you are comfortable to give. And don't receive more than you are prepared, be it abuse or demands, control or domination. Use your Rock & Water approach to enforce this.

The Wolves Within – a Cherokee Indian legend as metaphor for finding the balance point where peace and emotional harmony is strongest

A grandfather said to his grandson, who came to him with anger at a schoolmate who had done him an injustice, *"Let me tell you a story. I too, at times, have felt a great hate for those that have taken so much from me, have hurt and tortured my soul and spirit, they have no sorrow for what they do to me or to others. But hate wears you down, and does not hurt your enemy. It is like taking poison and wishing your enemy would die. I have struggled with these feelings myself many times."*

He continued, *"It is as if there are two wolves inside me; one is good and does no harm. He lives in harmony with all around him and does not take offence when no offence was intended. He will only fight when it is right to do so, and in the right way.*

"But the other wolf, ah! He is full of anger. The littlest thing will set him off into a fit of temper. He fights everyone, all the time, for no reason. He cannot think because his anger and hate are so great. It is helpless anger, for his anger will change nothing.

"Sometimes it is hard to live with these two wolves inside me, for both of them try to dominate my spirit."

The boy looked intently into his grandfather's eyes and asked, *"Which wolf wins, Grandfather?"*

The old man smiled and said, *"The one I feed, son, the one I feed."*

Author Unknown

Chapter 25 – Except: 'Astrology of Health: physical and psychological health in the natal and progressed charts'.

Earth Dominance in Health

(Image: *CELLARIUS, Andreas, "Haemisphaerium stellatum boreale antiquum"*. Map of the ancient Greek constellations of the northern sky. Original hand color. published in Amsterdam, 1708.)

Earth dominant people defend against the insecurity of change by stubbornly refusing to let go of control and closing down emotionally. They manage their insecurities by hoarding and collecting, they find comfort in controlling and stabilising their environment. Sameness is comfortable, change is frightening. They struggle against authority figures who try to take control of their possessions or push them to adapt too quickly.

Earth dominance describes someone who has a dominance of the earth element in their chart. An example is a stellium in an earth sign: Taurus, Virgo or Capricorn. It could also be a stellium in an earth house: 2nd, 6th or 10th house. I will also look for Sun or Moon in an earth sign or house and then consider what planets they conjunct as well. I always consider the Ascendant and Saturn's placement. All of these significators will describe the elementary dominance of the native. It takes practice but it certainly makes a difference when reading a chart to know what to look for in terms of elemental dominance.

According to Dr Sigmund Freud, the father of psychoanalysis, an earth dominance describes the Anal Psychosexual or psychological defence that develops around the time of a child's toilet training. Freud puts this stage at around the time when they discover that they can control their flow of urine and faeces. The issue is one of regulating and taking control of their pleasurable physical experiences.

When the child discovers that they can control their world they also want to do the same with their toileting. But no, now an authority figure takes control and claims the product of the child's pleasure, deficating. This can set up a power conflict between authority (the caregiver, mother, father or nanny) and the child.

When someone becomes fixated at this psychosexual stage, the earth defence becomes a power conflict with anyone in authority who tries to remove the native's control over their pleasure-giving possessions. This resistance is projected onto the school teacher, their manager, coworker or supervisor, police, neighbour and anyone else who tells them what to do and when to do it.

The earth dominant native is in charge of everything that brings pleasure, be it the toilet, bath, playing with toys or having fun with their friends. As they grow older they control and collect other gratifying things such as money, houses, cars, businesses, sport games, fun activities with friends, partners and lovers.

The earth dominance can become destructive when they fall in love and start dating. The earth person begins to oversee the giving and withholding of another crucial product: affection. They do this by controlling their loved one's access to house money, work contacts, schedules, shopping, access to the TV, computer, internet or phone and by limiting their partner's access to their friends and family. This creates a battleground in the marriage and I will often see the loser of this power struggle in my counselling sessions.

Earth strengths include the incredible stamina to work on a task, no matter how challenging it may be. Think of those postmen and women who set out to do their job be it rain, hail or sunshine. When something involves perseverance it is those with a strong earth element who will stick till it is done. They are reliable, resourceful and dependable in their desire to complete a task with maximum efficiency.

Earth dominance is seen with the luminaries (Sun and Moon) in earth signs or houses (2nd, 6th and 10th), and strongly placed Venus (particularly in Taurus), Saturn and Mercury (particularly in Virgo). For psychologists and counsellors, a planetary stellium in an earth house or sign will help you examine this defence fixation in therapy.

Other points to look for are planetary aspects, particularly conjunctions, to the luminaries Sun and Moon. For instance, Mercury conjunct Moon in Virgo will give an earthy emotional reaction. Saturn conjunct Sun or Moon is an extremely earthing conjunction that could build and strengthen self esteem.

Earth planets on the Angles, such as Saturn conjunct the Ascendant, are extremely powerful. So too is Saturn in an earth house (2nd, 6th or 10th house). Difficulties can arise with Venus and Mercury as they play a dual role in astrology rulerships. Venus rules both Taurus (passive) and Libra (active). Mercury rules both Gemini (active) and Virgo (passive). We would look at the whole chart to see if these two planets are in an active or passive state when determining elemental dominance too.

Saturn is the earthiest of the planets as he rules Capricorn and as such is extremely domineering and controlling of all your earthly pleasures. Saturn may not enjoy them but he certainly will control them.

You would also look for planetary patterns such as stelliums (group of four or more planets in one sign or house) in earth signs (Taurus, Virgo and Capricorn) as well as the earth houses. I consider a Grand Cross to be an earth planetary pattern. It has the power to contain and control the urges and instincts of the native. It is like a castle complete with moat and walls and helps the native control the external stressors from penetrating into their soft emotional centre. Unfortunately it can also restrict them from enjoying a lot of the pleasures and freedom of being in love or just participating in the fun of life.

In regards to health issues, hoarding can lead to a buildup of toxins in the body. Constipation is a health term we can substitute for hoarding. Problems arise when food is held in the intestines for too long, a result of the earthy impulse to hold on, a form of control. Earth signs learn that they can help remove these toxins by sharing their belongings and emotions, a good diet (vegan is always best), drinking plenty of water and some exercise each day.

Another facet of an earth dominance is skeletal structure and teeth. We would try to identify the powerful elements of Saturn and Capricorn here. Saturn however, is not always a sure-fire significator for skeletal or tooth problems, so we would have to consider a stellium in Capricorn and/or the 10th house. Stating that someone will have problems in this area because of a poorly aspected Saturn is way too general. That is why we always have a look at other factors and consider the entire chart not just single points.

I would consider a poorly placed Saturn and a stellium in the 10th house or Capricorn for bone issues only if the native is pregnant, seeking to fall pregnant or already has weak bones or osteoporosis. Astrologers seek to advise wisely without frightening people however people that are susceptible to breaks and osteoporosis can be warned appropriately.

My earthy friend, Laurie, who has a strong earth dominance in his chart, came home broken in body and spirit at the end of the 2nd

World War. After a lifetime of self-abuse, cigarettes, alcohol and shattered self-esteem, he was ready for the morgue. But Laurie was tough, he wouldn't let lymphatic cancer, heart disease, minimal circulation in his legs, skin cancers, blocked arteries in his neck and a stroke, not to mention the numerous tropical diseases, stop him from living.

On one of his down days Laurie read Ross Horne's book, 'Improving on Pritikin'. He decided to give it a go, it couldn't harm him he thought, he was already dying. Eating only fruit for the next two and a half years gave him back his life. His cancers disappeared; he had no need for his pacemaker; fresh blood circulated freely in his legs; he had no need for blood pressure tablets; he was free of the anxiety and the dark depths of depression that had plagued him since 1945.

Laurie was a living legend and demonstrated the healing power of raw fruit, vegetables and solid determination. I was honoured to have been there to assist in his psychological healing. He died at the ripe age of 82 years.

Book Reviews for 'Astrology of Health':

"Noel Eastwood is an amazing astrologer and gifted writer! I have never found so much good information about the astrology of health in any other book."

"Beautifully written book that looks at individuals likely health issues through their predominance of the elements in their charts. It looks at whether one has a Fire, Earth, Air or Water Dominance in their Natal Chart. Depending upon the leading element the

individual has, they will have certain strengths and weaknesses health wise. Written in an interactive conversational way between student and teacher it is entertaining and teaches the reader gradually over a number of lessons. Along the way it makes use of a number of case study charts to illustrate the lessons of elemental predominance with regards to Health. I know the elements are one of the cornerstones of Astrology. In understanding more about how their emphasis relates to one's health I found the book highly useful." DK

"I have just completed reading "Astrology of Health." I literally could not put it down. I learned so much!! By envisioning myself as silent observer at the table with Eastwood's student, I participated in each lesson. I am not an astrologer. Yet, I felt I examined each chart. I could clearly see the relationship between each astrological influence and how those influences manifested in each person's life. I had never thought about medical astrology at that depth nor had I clearly understood how generational charts reflected genetic, familiar medical and psychological themes and spiritual lessons. I was educated, informed, excited, and amazed!" CC

"This work by Noel Eastwood is a vital and necessary tool for all astrologers, beginners and professionals alike. His description of the Signs and their Elements (Air, Fire, Earth and Water) is exceptionally illuminating and unique, especially the way in which he describes the defences each element tends to erect. To know our weaknesses is surely one of the best tools we can possibly have at our disposal, and the clarity with which Noel describes and explains these weaknesses is without doubt, the most

insightful and enlightening available. But he doesn't stop there. He goes on to discuss and explain the various planetary and luminary effects that these have on our psychology and health, as well as giving vital information about the Angles (Asc./Desc., Midheaven/IC) with regard to health matters. In the 'Lessons' areas, peppered with actual charts, his discussions with his students are 'hands on' which gives even more clarity to this subject; and his style is 'natural', which is an invaluable quality that makes it easy reading. And be sure to read the Appendices, which are a true treasure of knowledge and understanding of this subject." S

Chapter 26 - Astrology, psychology and epilepsy

Sometimes astrology provides valuable clues for a therapist in the most difficult of circumstances.

Susan was under treatment from her psychiatrist and a clinical psychologist when she came to me for an astrology reading.

"I just go tingling all over my body, the blood drains from my face and I get hot and cold flushes. I get so scared I can't go out of the house for about 3 days and I can't even go to sleep. What can I do? I've already been to all the specialists and doctors in the city and I am desperate, can you please help me?"

During these attacks Susan would imagine or hallucinate faces, or more particularly one face, perhaps a man's. She couldn't describe it because she couldn't really see it, she just knew that it was there.

"The attacks seem to last only a few minutes and I lose all sense of place and time. If I look into the mirror I see this face and when I go to bed I am afraid I'll see it again. I also get a strange taste in my mouth and an unusual smell."

The description sounded at first glance like Panic Disorder (panic attacks) but a few discrepancies were entering the picture, like taste and smell which is more a sign of organic brain injury.

When asked if she could bring on the attack by thinking about it she said she couldn't, which is sometimes unusual in panic disorder. Then there was her dissociation and depersonalisation when she lost time and was in a space that she couldn't describe feeling as if she were out of her body while still in it. If she believed in UFOs perhaps she would have said that she had been abducted during this time but it only lasts for a minute or two.

An exploration of Susan's past history began to shed some light on her possible condition. As a one year old she had a fall and fractured her skull. As a 16 year old she smashed her head on the road when she jumped from a car when she thought the men in it meant to rape her. Then again her ex-husband repeatedly bashed her in the face and skull before she left him. So here are some possible causes of strange tastes and smells as well as dissociation and depersonalisation: traumatic brain injury.

Brain injury could possibly cause symptoms like Psychomotor Epilepsy which certainly describes Susan's symptoms well. However the CAT scans showed no brain lesions or injury. Was she born with it or did she need further scans like an EEG and MRI? Perhaps an answer could be found from her natal and transiting charts?

Susan's natal chart shows some interesting features the greatest being her Fixed Grand Cross which shows that she could be resistant to change. A Grand Cross lies in the realm of the unconscious and so Susan would have difficulty marshalling her healing resources due to its fixed nature.

Its composition is Mars, Uranus, Chiron and Jupiter all of which are strongly placed. Jupiter is in the conscious mind 3rd house opposing Mars in the higher conscious 9th house. Both houses involve mind issues and the planets described show the conflict and frustration Susan has when trying to connect consciously to her experiences. Then there is Uranus exact on the 12th house cusp, the house of the unconscious bringing up her deep psychological problems and throwing them into the fixed Grand Cross to be worked through in her conscious 3rd and 9th houses.

Uranus on the 12th, is not a good place for this young lady as it concentrates or channels too much psychical energy into consciousness, too much to think about can bring on panic attacks. Uranus is opposed by Chiron, the wounded healer, showing where she needs healing which is whole mind, body and spirit (6th house and Uranus on the 12th). Her weak constitution is shown by the 6th house placement of Chiron and the opening of the 12th house psyche into the 6th house suggests that she is susceptible to psychosomatic illnesses, illness brought on by psychological causes.

Virgo rising shows a predisposition to worry which we see is triggered later through transit by Mercury. Uranus trine Mercury is also high on the worry list as Uranus is bringing not only its intuition and sensitivity but the unresolved 12th house with it. Retrograde Mercury adds to our understanding of Susan's mental problems by showing us that Mercury issues often remain unresolved.

Mars is at the focal point of a Yod from Sun and North Node which adds anger as it too is involved with the fixed Grand Cross. It is anger that Susan presents when she is faced with her problem, her failed and miserable marriage and the beatings from her husband. Her parent's lack of care for the welfare of their daughter often throwing her out into the street at night and being forced to bring up her brothers and sisters while mum and dad drank and fought it out in the lounge room. In her early childhood transiting Pluto crawled slowly through her first house showing Susan's suffering through those early years of her life.

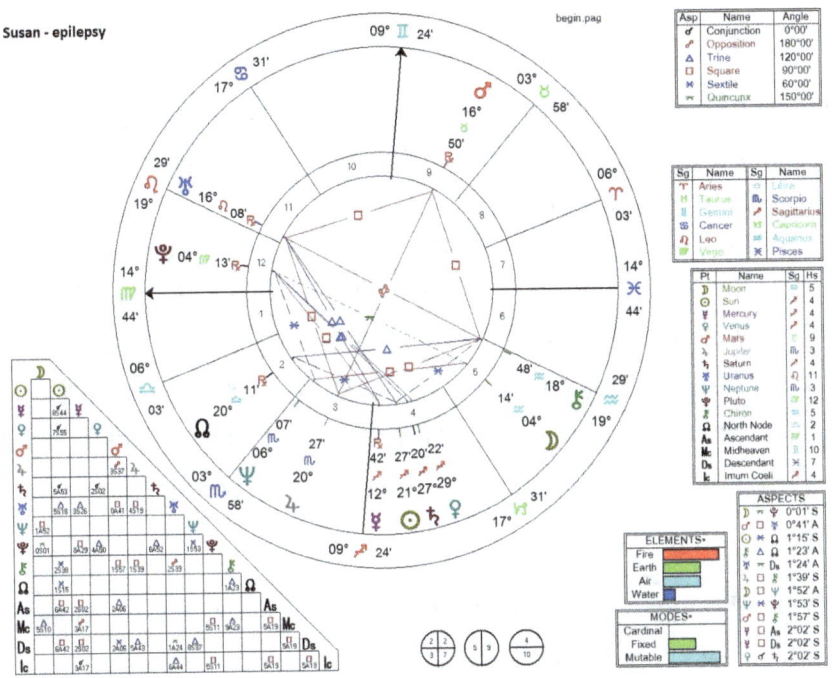

Susan - epilepsy

Saturn, never far away in cases of depression, is conjunct Sun and Venus previewing her failed marriage and the depression she experiences much of the time. Sun is in the happy and optimistic sign of Sagittarius, which is a God-send to ease her pain but there are too many other factors to really help. Pluto is in the 12th house close enough to the Ascendant to worry her, throwing her, again, into her deep unresolved psyche.

Susan's Moon in Aquarius adds tension and nervousness bringing her emotions to the raw surface when stressed. As for her dissociation and depersonalisation, Moon quincunx Pluto and squared by Neptune may account for a predisposition to hallucinations and psychological trauma. This could possibly predispose her to suffer from Post Traumatic Stress Disorder and Panic Disorder.

I have delineated the negative aspects of her chart to highlight what I am seeing and must consider when choosing which therapeutic approach to use.

Looking at her chart in such detail told me that Susan had some interesting characteristics of being a girl in need of therapy. Of course she also has a number of excellent qualities, she would have committed suicide by now if she didn't. Her strengths could be used in therapy to help harness her healing resources and to heal.

It was after her son was born that the symptoms began to show themselves. In her chart we would see Neptune is transiting Mercury and moving towards Sun causing some problems for her in coming to terms with the reality of her situation. She adores her son but admits that she also suffered from post-natal depression (PND) and had no support from her husband.

The Neptune transit to Mercury (ruler of her Ascendant) at the time she gave birth suggests that Susan could have succumbed to her natal predisposition to hallucinations, dissociation and depersonalisation, all of which are well in Neptune's realm.

At the time she attended psychotherapy (see transit chart below) Uranus was transiting her Moon and her emotions were running wildly into depression. An exhausted mother without support, beatings from her husband and the rising awareness that her son could end up living a life like her own were overwhelming. You would also look for Saturn to help explain the depression and there he is opposing her Mars challenging her ability to manage her frustrations and anger outbursts. This could also indicate she was currently the victim of domestic violence.

Susan came for a reading when these strange attacks overwhelmed her and she couldn't handle them with just the medication from her doctor. Her transits showed Uranus was adding levels of distress as it crossed her Moon over a full 12 months retrograding several times over that sensitive position.

Susan's North Node made a Return as well which could be seen as presenting an opportunity to resolve her situation. But the cards were stacked against her this time too as she moved from one therapist to another seeking an answer to her problems. Transiting Saturn remained sextile her Moon over the same 12 month period which also suggested an opportunity to heal. It was at this time when Susan came to see me to work on her problems, first with the natal chart which clearly explained her problems, and its triggers through transit and progression.

Susan made good progress when she did therapy on her trauma as a child. She went back to the hospital to heal the pain, dissociation and depersonalisation of her 1 year old self suffering from a fractured skull. A cold hospital ward, faces peering down at her in a state of reverie. It brought on a catharsis which suggests that she had found one of the symptoms of her condition – there was the face she saw, her surgeon's.

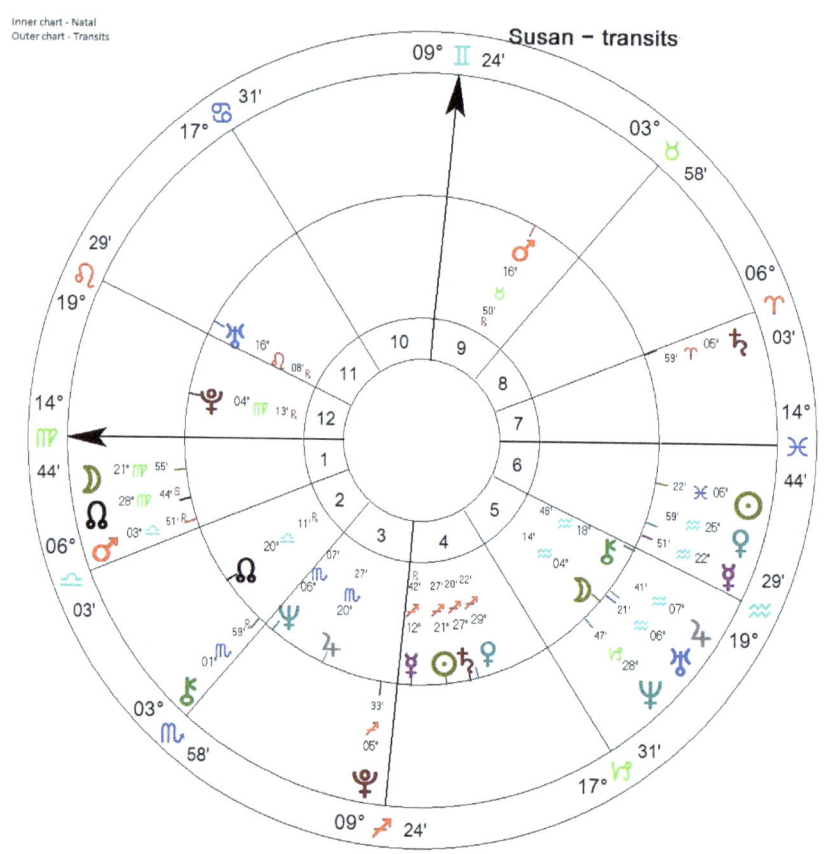

Susan was most likely suffering a traumatic brain injury that triggered a predisposition to psychological illness. It was most likely Psychomotor Epilepsy which is sometimes called Temporal Lobe Epilepsy.

The description of her symptoms fit the psychological picture of Psychomotor Epilepsy which also fits the description of her natal chart. A traumatic upbringing, traumatic marriage and three head injuries should be more than enough to tip the scales in favour of a predisposition to psychological illness plus epilepsy.

I believe that the planets indicate a person's personality traits and psychological disposition which appears as illness at certain times. I don't believe that planets cause, only indicate, a road map not the territory itself. We could describe a person's personality as a product of genetics and inherited characteristics, social exposure from school and friends and from a psychological base the result of upbringing. All these are shown in the natal chart followed by their consequences which we see in the transits, progressions and directions.

The last time I saw Susan she was under the care of her psychiatrist and heavily medicated. Psychotherapy and self hypnosis may help her manage triggers and stress but the underlying condition of epilepsy requires a multi-modal approach.

** This article appeared in the **Federation of Australian Astrologers** journal, 1997, Vol. 27, No. 2*

This series continues as ebook, audiobook and paperback. Further volumes will be announced in my Pluto's Cave newsletter.

Wishing you every success in your studies

Regards, Noel Eastwood, psychotherapist, astrologer, tarotist

December 2020

Australia

Free Psychological Astrology course

Study at your own pace and find out what your chart says about you. Learn how a psychotherapist uses the planets, signs, houses and the asteroid goddesses in his work. If you want to learn astrology this is a true gift.

www.plutoscave.com/freebies

About the Author

Noel Eastwood is a retired psychologist with over forty years professional experience in education, counselling and psychology. Now a full-time author, Noel shares his lifelong interests in psychotherapy, taoist meditation, tai chi, astrology and tarot. A gifted storyteller, his fiction and nonfiction works blend ancient wisdom and contemporary themes.

You can visit his website and subscribe to his newsletters on the many diverse topics above.

www.plutoscave.com

Other books by Noel Eastwood:

Psychological Astrology and the Twelve Houses – 2015 - also in audiobook

Psychological Astrology An Introduction – 2019 - also in audiobook

Self Hypnosis Tame Your Inner Dragons: Clinical and Psychic Use of Trance – 2016 - also in audiobook

Astrology of Health: Physical and Psychological Health in the Natal and Progressed Charts – 2016

The Fool's Journey Through The Tarot Major Arcana – 2017 also in audiobook

The Fool's Journey Through the Tarot Pentacles – 2018 - 2nd Edition - also in audiobook

The Fool's Journey Through the Tarot Swords – 2018 – also in audiobook

The Fool's Journey Through the Tarot Cups – due late 2020

The Fool's Journey Through the Tarot Wands – due 2021

www.ingramcontent.com/pod-product-compliance
Lightning Source LLC
Chambersburg PA
CBHW050316010526
44107CB00055B/2267